Sorry I ate all the cheez-its..."n

Brenden

BREAKING IN

Ben ~
Thanks for everything!

We will miss you! Thanks for everything!

We will miss you!

Brandi

♡ Betsy ☺

BREAKING IN

The Formula for Success in Entertainment

Evan Farmer

DALLAS • ATLANTA • NASHVILLE • LOS ANGELES

Andrea, Garrison, and Ford—this is for you!

BREAKING IN: THE FORMULA FOR SUCCESS IN ENTERTAINMENT

Copyright © 2012 by Evan Farmer

Published by
ISB Publishing
2128 Boll Street
Dallas, TX 75024 USA

ISBN 978-1-93-771700-1

Printed in the United States of America
10 9 8 7 6 5 4 3 2 1

CONTENTS

FOREWORD
by Kristin Chenoweth

Dear All Aspiring Artists,

You picked up the right book! For those of you who have followed my career, you have probably noticed that I like to do many things. I'm a singer, yes—you likely know that if you know who I am—but what I really do is entertain, whether it's on Broadway, at Carnegie Hall, in movies, on my (super-huge-smash-hit) TV sitcom, *Kristin,* or even in a few TV shows you may not have heard of, like *The West Wing, Pushing Daisies,* or *Glee.*

That's the key of the entertainment business success equation: entertain first! But what I have also found out the honest way is that no matter what passion drives you—from music to juggling fire—the realities of the entertainment industry remain roughly the same if you want to both work professionally and enjoy yourself while doing it. This book, written by my friend Evan, lays out the basic things you need to know going in.

Reading *Breaking In,* certain themes immediately hit home for me. First, it simply can't be about the fame for you if you truly want to have a real career and real happiness. In other words, you have to be truly passionate about the art itself and about entertaining people, and that needs to be enough. If you're not, it's way too easy to lose your way.

Second, even though you may have to audition at some point (depending on your discipline), trust me, this isn't a competition. I couldn't have gotten where I am without the support of my coworkers, colleagues, contemporaries (whatever you want to call them), and they couldn't have either!

You're gonna work hard—and I mean really, really hard—but a career in entertainment can also make for a ridiculously fun and unbelievably fulfilling life.

Last but not least, if one thing stands out above all else as an absolute must-have (especially in today's world), it's integrity. I love that Evan devotes a whole chapter to this. It's simply that important.

If you want to know more about how these things played a role my life and career, please also read my book, *A Little Bit Wicked: Life, Love, and Faith in Stages.* (Please read it anyway, Evan would really like you to!)

But even if you read a hundred or more biographies and somehow managed to interview a few hundred successful artists, I'd almost guarantee that you'd hear the exact same themes that are in this book repeated over and over; I see it everyday, all around me. That's what makes this a great handbook—it covers much of what took so many years for so many of the most successful artists to figure out the hard way.

Will it prevent you from learning or relearning some of these things yourself? I hope not! That's the joy and richness of life. But what's in these pages can definitely take the sting out of some things and certainly will send you in the right direction from the start. And, truthfully, that may be the biggest battle of all.

Above all, do everything with passion, and your star will shine!

Love,
Kristin

INTRODUCTION

In 1995, I graduated from Tulane University with a degree in business consulting and . . . with zero intention of ever consulting any businesses. I did, however, desperately want to: act in movies, on stage, and on television; record a hit album and tour as a rock star; and maybe do some modeling.

Until graduation day, however, the moment at which I was generally expected to head out into the world and actually *do something,* I had pretty much considered those dreams my "dirty little secret."

Finally, one night—in the middle of the night—after no fewer than fourteen consecutive sleepless nights, grappling with my future and a million conflicting expectations (most of them my own), I packed my car and started driving toward New York City. As the sun rose outside the passenger-side window somewhere just north of Alabama, I realized that I had officially decided to pursue my outlandish dreams.

If I had told most people around me what I planned—essentially, starting over after five expensive years of intense study—and the time frame in which I planned to do it—five years (for no other reason than I figured the year 2000 was a good time to "arrive")—they would have laughed loudly in my face. In fact, one friend did just that, so I told very few.

At five-foot-nine (models are almost always at least six feet tall) and twenty-five pounds overweight, with no significant acting talent, zero formal training save for a few voice lessons, and absolutely no professional experience, I set off for the Big Apple.

By 1999, only four years later, I had modeled for a billboard ad, landed a TV ad campaign for Mountain Dew, and spent a year starring in the Off-Broadway production of *The Fantasticks* (the longest-running musical in history). I had also completed a stadium tour with Ha-Ha (Russia's most successful pop group in history), landed my first major studio film role alongside Christian Bale in *Shaft Returns* (starring Samuel L. Jackson), and filmed the lead role in MTV's first-ever made-for-TV movie: *2GE+HER*. The success of that MTV project would spawn two gold albums, a wildly successful follow-up TV series, my own doll for sale in toy stores, and a second stadium tour opening up for pop music's biggest star of the day: Britney Spears.

By the age of twenty-seven, within four years of graduating college and exactly one year shy of my arbitrary five-year timeline, I was wealthy (by many standards) and had accomplished *literally* every goal I had set out to achieve in that time frame.

Meanwhile, many, if not most, of the friends I had graduated with were toiling away on the bottom of some corporate ladder in a cubicle somewhere "playing it safe."

How did I do it? I used the simple and universal formula for success I learned from the most successful artists and most successful successes in history: the same one I will spell out in this book.

By 2010, exactly fifteen years later, armed with the same simple formula I used to achieve that long list of dreams right out of college, I've added:

- An unofficial world record (in 2008, I built an airplane in eleven days and flew it solo across the United States in another nine)
- A role as the young version of "Number 2," the character originated by Robert Wagner (also portrayed by Rob Lowe),

in *Austin Powers in Goldmember* (among the highest-grossing comedy films of all time)

- Two number-one music videos
- Becoming a published ASCAP songwriter
- No fewer than twenty more television shows, including hosting the Emmy-nominated home makeover show *While You Were Out*
- Being established as an in-demand public speaker, fetching $10,000 or more per appearance
- Founding a successful real estate/home renovation business
- Cofounding a television production company
- Becoming the host and consulting producer of Country Music Television's flagship show: *CMT's Top 20 Countdown* (since I took over in 2009, it has achieved its highest recorded ratings since it first aired in 2001)
- Cohosting *CMT Radio Insider*—a weekly nationally syndicated radio show

Borrowing from Anthony Robbins (after listing his own achievements):

I don't tell you this to impress you, but to impress *upon you* that if I can repeatedly achieve these things without any natural born advantages, then so can you!

In fact, history is overflowing with names of those who have achieved far more while hailing from far less likely circumstances and overcoming far greater challenges; people like Oprah Winfrey, Beethoven, Walt Disney, Sidney Poitier, Harrison Ford, Jerry Seinfeld, Oliver Stone, Marilyn Monroe, John Grisham, Lucille Ball, Ozzy Osborne, J. K. Rowling, Steven Spielberg, Mark Wahlberg, Charles Schultz, Elvis Presley, the Beatles, or Madonna, to name just a few.

There are infinitely more names of those who have achieved great things without becoming well-known public figures. I have spent the better part of my life studying people from both camps.

What I didn't initially realize when I graduated from college and headed out from New Orleans toward New York City in the middle of the night was that my very expensive degree preparing me to consult Fortune 500 companies was not wasted—as I think many people close to me had assumed.

On the contrary, my studies directly translated into me not only beating the seemingly ludicrous odds in a profession typically believed to be reserved for the "lucky few" with "loads of talent," but to do so time and time again, in nearly every mutually exclusive genre of entertainment.

Looking back, I believe that perhaps my greatest achievement was my ability to make a regular day job out of a profession that is typically littered with single chances. In short: *I know how to break in!*

I took this same formula and applied it with equal success in every other venture I've tackled *outside* entertainment. Some of these efforts include: starting businesses, buying real estate, giving lectures, writing a book, advancing philanthropies of significant meaning to me, and doing things simply to see if I can, like . . . building a plane.

How did I achieve all of these things? I simply applied the same principles I learned from the Fortune 500s and the successful artists I've studied to the business of "me."

These just so happen to be the same principles used by literally every significant successful individual throughout history, from Henry Ford to Harrison Ford.

But you don't need to complete 127 credits from Tulane University or read a thousand biographies to learn and use these same tools. I'll be the first to say that the vast majority of my formal education has been lost, totally forgotten, or was fluff in the first place. I only remembered the simple entertainment formula because . . . it was so simple and happened to be *repeated* over and over again in almost every single story I read from some of the most successful entertainers in history.

What I have always wanted to know as I read each success story was this:

1. What did they do that was different from "regular" people?
2. How could I do what they did?
3. What were the common qualities that all successful entertainers shared that unsuccessful entertainers didn't possess?

I reasoned that if I learned these three things, I had a bona fide road map to becoming successful at anything. The very question I kept asking became my answer:

How do most successful entertainers become successful?

1. They *also* asked what made other successful entertainers successful!
2. They also learned what mistakes *other* successful entertainers made along the way.
3. They also went out and did more or less those same things, minus the mistakes, and got the same results. And they got *even better* results if they happened to make an improvement or two along the way!

This is the broad-strokes ARMS formula:

Ask + Repeat – Mistakes = Success
A + R – M = S

The key is getting the right answers (which means asking the right questions) and then figuring out how to make the right improvements along the way. That's what I will show you. Many people, sadly, just wait to be told everything. That's why so many people are average.

Luckily, as it turns out, there is no shortage of über-successful people willing and eager to share their story. On the other end of the spectrum, there is a never-ending cadre of "teachers" out there who are willing to take your money. They dispel "wisdom" but have never actually practiced what they preach with any success.

I learned, for example, that most acting teachers have very little, if any, professional acting experience. I also discovered, after my first experience investing and losing much of my hard-earned money at age twenty-seven, that most stockbrokers are . . . broke. I quickly realized that the *source* of information was everything. Did I take acting classes? Yes. They're a great place to learn the craft. But I didn't just want to be a good actor—I wanted to be a working actor!

This often-overlooked distinction, which we've been all but trained to ignore in formal schooling, has been the crux of my lifelong research, both as my undergraduate focus and continuing as a post-college obsession.

When I first sought to break into film, I didn't call the most reputable acting teacher in New York for advice. Instead, I read or watched every interview or biography I could find about Tom Cruise, Rob Lowe, and Harrison Ford, to name just a few.

Hell, even before I bought my first New York City apartment for a mere $120,000 (extremely cheap by NYC standards) I read everything I could find written by or about Donald Trump, Steve Wynn, and Robert Kiyosaki. Overkill? Maybe, but I got a great apartment for a great deal, and I still own it to this day!

After a while, a few distinct themes and character traits started to emerge and continuously reappear among every successful entertainer (and successful person for that matter) that I studied, and my questions were quickly answered.

For example: Are all super-successful people fearless? No, but they all *learned* to be confident. Are all super-successful people social animals? No, but they are all great networkers.

Did any one of them just get lucky? No, in fact quite the opposite: every single one of them took an enormous amount of action to get where they are, and all of them endured many of what most people would call "catastrophic failures" along the way.

Breaking In is the result of studying and replicating the universal methods and characteristics of the most successful entertainers and successful people in history and is based on the success I've had in applying those key distinctions to my own life. It's also about how to study and replicate successful strategies in any field of interest.

If you (or someone you care about) are considering a career in entertainment and are hungry to take your career and your life to the next level, then this book is for you!

FACTS

The first section of this book is designed to help you make a few basic assessments about yourself as a potentially viable working entertainer and to begin to make a few key distinctions between what you already know about the entertainment industry and what you may have been incorrectly led to believe about this industry. The only way to do this is to deal in facts. And there are more than a few myths about this industry that need to be dispelled.

Some myths are embraced by aspiring artists themselves as security blankets, such as the notion that in order to succeed in entertainment you need to be somehow "discovered." This myth lets us feel better about ourselves for not succeeding because it provides an easy excuse (bad luck) for not really doing the hard work, taking uncomfortable risks, putting in the time, and having the patience that's required to go the distance.

Some myths are simply created as forms of entertainment unto themselves, as seen in tabloids and entertainment news shows. Regardless of where they come from, all of them can potentially derail your otherwise sincere efforts if you don't understand them and identify them as myths.

The most important facts to understand, however, are the ones about you. That's what chapter 3, Is This for You, is all about. This chapter, as you'll likely notice, is less about *Are you talented enough?* than it is about whether or not you have the drive and personality best suited for this profession.

The rest of this book is about becoming and/or fine-tuning yourself into the type of person you need to be in order to succeed.

Myths, Lies, and the Secrets of the Über-Celebrities

FIRST OF ALL—congratulations! If you've picked up this book, you're probably interested in pursuing some aspect of the entertainment industry—the most exciting and fulfilling career imaginable, in my opinion—or someone you care about is. The best news is that there has never been a better time to get into the business of entertainment than now. Why? With the advent of cable and the rise of online entertainment, there have never been more opportunities to work in and market creative pursuits in the history of our country; and the fact is that the United States offers more of these jobs than any other country in the world!

In fact, not only does the United States lead the world in every aspect of entertainment—film, television, music, and style—but it's just about the only thing left (other than debt) that America exports more than it imports.

Right off the bat, these facts dispel the first pervasive myth about the entertainment industry, and that is:

Myth #1: Entertainment is a field reserved for only the most talented, beautiful, and connected.

There is simply way too much demand for talented artists out there for the current talent pool to fill! All that is required to be a successful entertainer these days is the ability to create a demand for yourself, much the same way Apple created a demand for the iPod, which in turn created the demand for high-quality, inexpensive, and downloadable digital music. Before the iPod, we all thought CDs were just fine, remember? We never knew we *needed* ten thousand songs at our fingertips . . . until it became an option. This book will guide you in the process of creating a demand for "you," a product that the world didn't know it needed . . . until now!

Innovation Is Easier Than You Think

Entertainment has always been a field of innovation, whether it's Kid Rock introducing the world to a whole new genre of Rap-Rock, Jim Carrey's over-the-top physical comedy, Steven Spielberg's special effects, or Mariah Carey's five-octave vocal range. But while each genre-changing, seminal figure of entertainment had to literally create a new way, a new style, and a better brand to become the giants they are, it's easier than you might think to create a gigantic demand for a reliable, consistent, interesting, and fun-to-work-with performer in any discipline: a demand for people like me.

In fact, today more than ever, that demand already exists. Actually, the demand is enormous! Tabloids are filled with the names of those who have oversaturated the market with the opposite qualities—i.e., egocentric, vacuous, drug-addicted, difficult to work with, and above all . . . unreliable! Some of these people have literally made it virtually impossible to be rehired, as the insurance premiums on them cost more than their own salaries!

And for every breakthrough artist like the ones I mentioned, there are thousands of very well-paid, very well-respected, and—most importantly—very fulfilled artists who have found tremendous success *without* natural gifts or advantages. They, like me, got there using some variation of this same time-tested formula.

Discovering the Formula for Breaking In

When I moved to New York City to start my career in entertainment, I knew from the get-go that I was not the most-talented, best-trained, best-looking, or smartest guy trying to break into the industry. Nor was I the benefactor of nepotism or endless family wealth capable of supporting my dream. In fact, within a week of moving to New York (and selling my car for a month's worth of groceries) I could easily count five waiters and bartenders (a synonym for entertainer in the city) working alongside of me who were, without any shadow of a doubt, better actors, better singers, better looking, and better trained than I was. Of those five people, and of the hundreds of people I climbed alongside over the following few years, I'm one of the very few who actually made a successful career in entertainment.

It was this realization, which occurred as I looked back over a long, diverse, and successful career, that drove me to sit down and write this book. I wanted to know why I succeeded when others did not. I wondered if there was something about how I approached this business that allowed me to repeatedly break into several different—even mutually exclusive—segments of entertainment, when all around me far superior talents failed at breaking in to even *one* arena.

I started to list the things that I believed were critical to my success, and I started comparing notes with other successful entertainers and what I found was that several repeated themes began to materialize into a "formula."

One of the reasons I was able to consistently find work, for example, is that I approached the industry from a different perspective than the many, far-more-talented people around me who were "out to give it a shot." I wasn't "out to give it a shot," I

was there to do it . . . period. I never *tried* to succeed in entertainment; I *decided* to be a successful entertainer. There was,
and still is, no grey area in between these two approaches for me.

This drive for success was evident from the get-go in two
other actors I would frequently see at auditions early on who
went on to achieve great success: Zach Braff *(Scrubs)* and Ed
Norton *(Primal Fear),* and in Kristin Chenoweth, whose multi-
genre star rose like a rocket shortly after she left the cast of the
very same production of *The Fantasticks* that I was soon to join.
Even back then, before any of us had any modicum of success,
everyone could tell that these three would eventually succeed—
it was obvious.

At some point, looking over the list I compiled, I identified
one critical distinction that stands out over everything else. If
Breaking In has one overall theorem, it's this:

**Successful people *think* differently than unsuccessful
people.**

It was an alarmingly simple epiphany. It was something I
had always lived but had taken for granted as something of critical significance. Although this concept isn't new, I had never
seen it specifically applied to the context of the entertainment
industry where, based on the amazing talent I saw waiting
tables around me, it was desperately needed.

I think this theorem ultimately relates directly to the many
myths that the popular media sells us about successful entertainers, suggesting just about every reason for someone's success, such as exceptional ability, luck, or the "it" factor, while
completely ignoring and glossing over the far less sexy but more
likely reasons, such as confidence, drive, decisiveness, believing in themselves, and a lot of focused hard work.

And that's what *Breaking In* is, in a nutshell: a diagram of
how to think, along with the traits, skills, and actions necessary
in order to succeed in this business, regardless of how gifted
you are (a very poor barometer for artistic success, by the way).

In fact, rarely will you ever hear a truly successful person attribute their achievements to natural ability. Not Will Smith, not Oprah, not Harrison Ford, not Madonna. This book is a focused look at what entertainers who have succeeded at their level *do* attribute their successes to; the same formula I have used to achieve what I have always dreamed of.

Before I dive in from the beginning, let me share one other realization from my list that stood out:

Successful people work harder than unsuccessful people.

Combine this with the statement above and you get:

Successful people work harder at working smarter than unsuccessful people because they *think* differently.

Along with these revelations are a few more myths that need to be exposed right off the bat:

Myth #2: Huge stars are "discovered" all the time.

Trust me when I tell you that the myth of being discovered is just that: a myth! In the freakishly rare instances in which someone seems to have been plucked from obscurity while minding their own business, there's always far more to the story than meets the eye. Even if there are any true "discoveries" out there, you'd still have a greater chance of winning the lottery than of this ever happening to you. Besides, there is a direct and proven correlation between how one gets to the top and how long one stays there.

Most of the stories we've all heard are simply the product of clever marketing and publicity, or the "David Letterman Story" as I like to call it, because it's perfect talk-show banter that's merely designed to make a person's rise to fame seem more exciting. For everyone *living* the dream, there's someone *selling* it!

Trust me, every "overnight success" that I know of spent years working extremely hard and working smarter to make it happen.

Myth #3: You've gotta have the "IT" factor.

Hear me now: The "IT" factor is bullsh*IT*! While a lot of lip service is paid to the notion that some people are just blessed with the IT factor, I personally don't buy IT. It's an awfully convenient label that has been historically endowed upon successful entertainers, almost entirely after the fact, and it plays into our fantasy that "some people are just blessed," thereby excusing us for our own shortcomings. In other words: it's designed to make us feel better, and IT makes for good conversation . . . period.

Instead, I believe IT is simply a combination of a few things: drive, decisiveness, believing in yourself, and a lot of focused hard work. Someone who is driven, believes in what he or she is doing, and is crystal clear in his or her focus usually appears very confident. We tend to group all of these qualities together and label this charisma, a somewhat less sexy synonym for IT.

I believe, however, that IT *can* be learned and therefore can be taught. I'm living proof. I was not endowed with charisma or the "Who's that guy?" gift. Myself aside, just look at the hundreds of ridiculously successful artists who only have a modicum of natural talent at best, or who overcame tremendous challenges, be they physical, financial, or circumstantial, to get where they are. I've already listed a bunch of names from the entertainment world, but let's just examine one of these seminal figures for a second: Oprah Winfrey.

Oprah is certainly one of the most influential entertainers in the world, despite growing up poor, having been sexually abused as a child, struggling with obesity, being African American and female in the very male-dominated and once very-white business of television news—especially in 1973 when she started out! Wow! This pretty much negates any excuse I've ever heard come out of someone's mouth as to why they couldn't achieve their dreams! If you've ever watched a few episodes of *Oprah,* you'll also hear her describe success as being pretty simple.

Already I can hear you saying "Wait a minute . . . if it's so simple, then why doesn't everyone know how to do it?" Well, to be honest, I think almost everyone does know or has, at the very least, heard most of what you'll read here at one point in their lives already.

Two realities are at play here. The first is the fact that in today's information age, we are constantly bombarded with so much information that it becomes difficult to sort out and identify only the most useful and practical information. In other words, we easily become overwhelmed by all of the advice and opinions, often to the point of paralysis.

The other reality is that even though it's very simple, it still requires a lot of effort to implement and most people are either too lazy, too scared, or have been brainwashed into a mindset of failure, believing everything to be a competition—i.e., you either succeed or fail. Ergo, someone else succeeds in your place. This couldn't be further from the truth. Which brings me to the next myth.

Myth #4: Entertainment is a competition.

This brainwashing, so to speak, is perhaps the biggest reason that some of the most talented people in the world will never get beyond waiting tables.

In today's world, there are critical distinctions between what successful entertainers believe and understand and what the majority of us are constantly being taught in school and continues to be reinforced in today's society. Successful entertainers understand that success does *not* require someone else to fail.

Our formal education and social systems (born out of the industrial age) still train and prepare us to learn a specific vocation, get a job by being better than the other guy, work for someone else, and, most critically, avoid making mistakes at all costs! This paradigm encourages the idea that everything in life is a competition and not a team sport. Just think of how we're administered exams: no helping each other! And above all, try not to make too many mistakes or else you'll fail and be humiliated!

This archaic, schoolhouse concept is even demonstrated in the realm of TV entertainment. Reality competition shows like *American Idol, America's Got Talent,* and *So You Think You Can Dance?,* to name a few, act to reiterate the myth that to achieve success you must take the test (i.e., audition each week in front of millions), ace it (i.e., move on to the next round), and avoid any mistakes that will serve only to humiliate you, sometimes permanently and on a national stage, thereby cementing your utter failure in entertainment.

Shows like *American Idol* also serve up the idea that becoming a successful artist is a one-in-a-million shot (even if you're really talented), and that impossible dream is why the show is fun and interesting.

The reality of this business, though, is that it's tedious and often boring, frustrating, and repetitious, but many parts of it are also somewhat predictable! It won't likely happen for you in the span of a season, but any real success—in any field—takes time.

If you have been a viewer of one of these shows, you may have noticed that most of the show's cast-offs are rarely heard from again. Heck, we usually only hear from the winners for a few months after their victory! This is not because they're not talented enough (as we are expected to believe) but primarily for these three simple reasons:

1. They viewed their rejection or frustration at not becoming an instant overnight sensation as a failure.

2. They never built a background or foundation on which to take the next necessary steps for success, once they had a little exposure.

3. They gave up. Period. Even many of the winners chose not to be the last one standing in the end, once their fame-crutch was taken away.

I've long since adopted a mantra that speaks to this last point. It comes from an interview I read with Harrison Ford, who spent over a decade as a carpenter in LA trying to make a name for himself in acting. During that period of time, he had been discouraged multiple times, even being told after his first film by movie execs that he simply didn't have what it took to be a star. But he kept going, citing the law of attrition as one of the keys to success in entertainment; in other words, *the last one standing wins.*

Another thing is, these shows always seem to eliminate some of the best contestants. It'd be impossible to say for sure, but I'd be willing to bet that some of the biggest innovators in entertainment history wouldn't have stood a chance in those arenas. Imagine Mick Jagger as a contestant on *American Idol*—that is, if he even made it past the first round! What would the judges have told him as he worked a little "Start Me Up," gyrating awkwardly—the same gyrations, by the way, that are studiously copied by millions of singers and bands since the Rolling Stones? Never mind the idea that you have to look like a supermodel to succeed. Which takes us back to *Myth #1: Entertainment is a field reserved for only the most talented, beautiful, and connected.*

Airbrushed magazines and tabloids (the printed kind and the televised kind) are the single biggest sellers of this myth for one reason and one reason only: money.

Tabloids focus on the pretty people in order to sell us a fantasy for escapism, but of course they do not provide anything close to a representation of the truly successful entertainers out there. Rags and gossip shows simply keep us worshiping celebrity for celebrity's sake, all the while reminding us that although we're beneath them, we can be like them . . . if we drink Coca-Cola, wear Armani, carry Louis Vuitton, take this weight-loss pill, blah, blah, blah.

If you made a comprehensive list of successful entertainers, you'd run out of pretty people awfully quick and you'd find that non–supermodel types make up the vast majority of entertainers—people like Lyle Lovett, Steven Tyler, Rosie O'Donnell, Steve Buscemi, Al Roker, Oprah Winfrey, and of course, Mick Jagger. That list goes on and on and on! They're definitely not your traditional supermodel group, yet they are super-successful.

I want to be crystal clear: this is not meant to be an indictment of the system. After all, the system is ultimately built upon advertising, which will hopefully pay for your yacht one day. Rather, this is my attempt to illustrate how the system has brainwashed us into thinking in terms of competition, scarcity, the IT factor, and perhaps the most damaging myth of all:

Myth #5: Making mistakes and taking chances lead to long-term suffering.

Later, I'll share some techniques for managing rejection, perceived failure, and the fear that comes with risk. This is an industry that, perhaps more than any other, requires you to manage these emotions—the most successful people even learn how to use them to their advantage.

Risk, however, is unavoidable if you want to succeed. In fact, the biggest rewards come to those who take the biggest risks. *Breaking In* will help you choose the right ones and mitigate the biggest risks to your advantage.

The first step is seeing beyond these myths and, instead of playing into the system, focusing your attention on some basic truths. In the *business* of entertainment, you are an entrepreneur, a business owner, a salesperson, and an artist—i.e., the product you're selling . . . in that exact order of importance!

Not only are there different rules for entrepreneurs, but success as an entrepreneur requires an entirely different emotional construct and belief system. The successful entrepreneur understands two critically important principles:

1. The route to success is not a competition or about grabbing a piece of the pie, it's about *making your own pie.*

2. There is no such thing as failure, only *information* that we can use to our benefit.

In other words, our biggest competition is not out there. It's in our own heads! *Breaking In* will follow these two truths along with some critical rules to live by in order to get out of your own way and achieve success.

Rule 1: Decide today to challenge old beliefs.

How to Use This Book

AS YOU MAY have already noticed, this book is about becoming or *being* the type of person that achieves success in the entertainment field. There are no tricks, shortcuts, or secrets to real success, and this book begins with that truth. It's my opinion that anyone who tells you something different is just selling you something or wants something from you.

It's also important to know what this book is *not.* It's not about which agent you should choose; what your headshot, reel, or résumé should look like; or which school to go to. These variables and a million others just like them change far too quickly for a list to be useful. Any specific requirements in your chosen branch of entertainment will often be completely different tomorrow, much less by the time this book or any book could get published. The two best ways to find those answers will always be asking around (always remember to consider the source) and the Internet.

The good news is that there really aren't that many specific variables to figure out, and even those you'll need to be current on for the most part will pale in comparative importance to what you will find in this book. Why? Because it's the person who gets the job in the end, not the head shot, agent, or school! And being that person is what this book is all about.

The Nuts and Bolts

Breaking In was designed as a handbook, one that is meant to be read from beginning to end. The main part of the book consists of four distinct sections: *Think, Traits, Skills,* and *Action,* which can be referenced easily at different stages in your career or at roadblocks you may encounter along the way.

Each chapter concludes with a rule that summarizes the chapter's key points. Taken together, these make up the blue-print of *Breaking In.*

It is my goal that down the line, as you run into stumbling blocks, obstacles, and rough patches, you will go back and reread the portions and stories in this book that relate to your situation to find guidance, clarity, or even just a little additional motivation.

If nothing else, I suggest bookmarking chapter 7, Ten Questions All Successful Artists Ask. These ten questions alone will help you provide the answers you need for yourself in any given situation.

But Please Don't Stop Here!

If I have achieved one thing with this book, I hope it is that I will have inspired you to seek more information and answers for yourself, as *you* are the single best provider of the best advice that you will ever need to succeed.

Throughout this book, you will find references, concepts, and passages from other authors, as well as a fairly lengthy list of additional sources for information in the appendix. I have personally read each and every one of the books mentioned (several times actually) and I encourage you to read as many of them as you can while seeking out other material that speaks to you. Why? Because, even though I have synthesized many of their critical concepts here, it would be impossible in just a few hundred pages to elaborate further on each principle I mention, nor is there enough room here to cover every great concept these authors offer in the first place.

Besides, the vast majority of these books were written by people who have spent their entire lives in search of the answer(s) to one question: Why do people succeed? And each has a different way of communicating what they have discovered than I do. I assure you that you will benefit tremendously from their perspective and approaches, some of which may resonate with you and your learning style better than this book might. Nonetheless, all of them were written by people who have achieved success—even if it wasn't in the specific category of entertainment.

Lastly, I imagine there will be two types of people who read this book: people who are looking for a few quick concepts, tips, and time-saving direction and people who are so hungry for success in this business that they will seek out and consume every bit of available information that will give them a decisive advantage.

This book, I believe, will provide both groups with what they are looking for. The latter group will greatly increase their odds of becoming superstars in their field and will get there much faster. This never-ending quest for improvement will take much, if not all, of the luck right out of the equation.

In my experience, these two groups often represent the difference between the *doers* and the *wannabes*.

Some wannabes get close and may even occasionally win a round or two. Doers win in the end every time.

The first choice you must make is to decide whether or not this career is for you—it's not for everybody! I suggest that you read this book all the way through before you ultimately decide, as only the big picture will help you truly understand what it takes to succeed in entertainment. If, after reading, you have decided it is for you, I suggest that you use this book as a reference to keep yourself on track and to save critical time on your journey to success.

Is This for You?

The 90/10 Rule: Show Business Is 90 Percent Business and 10 Percent Show

The American Psychological Association has developed sophisticated personality tests designed to give you an idea of where your strengths lie and even to suggest what types of pursuits you should avoid. I took one my sophomore year in college, and it pointed me toward both the creative arts and the military. This confused me to say the least, and my reaction at that time was to continue studying architecture and taking powerhouse electives like scuba-diving and tennis.

Only years later, after having worked in entertainment, did the military reference make sense to me. Although I am an expressive and rebellious artist, another facet of my personality is that I crave structure and thrive in areas that require self-discipline. Unfortunately, structure and discipline are commonly thought to stifle creativity, and in some cases this is certainly true.

But once I realized that show business is only 10 percent show and 90 percent business, I was able to see how the disciplined and structured side of me really played a major role in my ability to succeed. In this way, the business of entertainment suits my opposing personality traits perfectly, even if an internal war is often being waged inside of me as a result.

To be clear, I'm not suggesting that you have to go out and take the same personality test I did (though it couldn't hurt). And even if you did, the results wouldn't tell you if this business is right for you anyway—only you can do that.

To help you make this decision, however, I've put together a few questions that should shed some light on your choice based on what I came to see as the realities of the industry:

Do you believe it's possible to succeed?

Even if you're skeptical that you too could become the next Brad Pitt, Julia Roberts, Bono, Madonna, Baryshnikov, or Steven Spielberg, that's ok. You do need, at the very least, to believe it's possible. If you don't believe it's possible right now, I will provide you with some tools to hopefully change your perspective. If, after my best attempt to do so, you still don't believe it's possible, then frankly this industry is not for you.

How you approach anything will always determine your outcome. Henry Ford, father of the modern-day assembly line and founder of the Ford Motor Company said it best: "Whether you think you can or think you can't—you are right."

In the next chapter, I will expand further on the importance and power of this fact, but for now a quick self-check will do. Answer the following question for yourself: *Can I become the next [insert your idol here]?* If you answered yes—or even maybe—you're off to a great start. If you answered no, then immediately throw this book as hard as you can at your TV, guitar, or DVD collection, because that's about as close to being a part of them professionally as you'll ever get.

> Whether you think you can or think you can't—you are right.
> —*Henry Ford*

Are you driven?

More than any other factor, having an all-consuming desire will determine not only how successful you will be at meeting your goals, but also how quickly you'll meet them.

Driven people win, win big, and win first. One of the best documentary-style shows I have ever seen that illustrates this very point is called . . . wait for it . . . *Driven.* It first appeared on VH1 in 2002 and chronicled the careers of contemporary music success stories through the lenses of drive, determination, and raw stamina. From the show's website:

> *Driven* brings the music world's biggest pop icons' unknown pasts to life with footage that the public has never seen, plus interviews with those special people who played integral roles in their development as artists and individuals, providing a rare glimpse at what they were really like. There's no such thing as an overnight success—over time, like a jigsaw puzzle, pieces are added, small breakthroughs are made, and eventually the picture of a pop star begins to take shape. *Driven* traces that process from childhood to the first glimmer of stardom, through the eyes of those who knew the artist best and helped play pivotal roles in their development—teachers, family members, friends, and creative partners. With each episode of *Driven* dedicated to a single artist, the show looks at the stars' blueprints for success and what propelled them to achieve it despite the obstacles that lay in their paths.

Perhaps the most interesting aspect of *Driven* was that it did not feature the typical glorification of talent, but rather focused on how every one of these people, with the sole exception of having unprecedented drive were, and are, just like everyone else.

Although *Driven* focused on singers, the same principles

apply to every discipline in entertainment across the board. In fact, I believe that if it is ever proven that a single "gene" can be isolated to determine success, it will be the gene that determines drive. Of course billions of social factors determine the individual drive of any given human being, and this is good news, because once you find a way to latch onto and harness its power, nothing will stand in your way, period.

One caveat: There is often a fine line between drive and obsession. Even in many success stories, that line has been crossed. It's imperative that you first establish a healthy definition of success for yourself, which I'll help you do. After all, what are the points of fame and fortune if they come with drugs, alcohol, depression, paranoia, isolation, or early death?

Do you want to be famous?

The lure of fame is certainly a very powerful motivator for many people, especially in the fame-crazed world we live in today. In much the same way, crack cocaine is a great motivator for users to acquire vast sums of money. Pure and simple, fame (by today's standards) is a drug. It is on this point that I provide my only warning regarding your goals.

> The talent of success is nothing more than doing what you can do well and doing well whatever you do without thought of fame.
> —Henry Wadsworth Longfellow

At some point during the last decade or so, the definition of *fame* changed dramatically. Fame used to be defined as "the condition of being known or talked about by many people *on account of notable achievements.*" But now, those last few words have been forgotten, and the new definition of fame is simpler: "The condition of being known or talked about by many people." Period.

I personally believe that reality television has had a huge impact on this destructive new "cultural value," as networks, eager to cash in on the vulnerable and fame-addicted, began luring people into "social experiment shows" by promising fame and then plying them with high-stress scenarios (and sometimes alcohol) and generally encouraging ridiculous behavior.

The classic reality TV formula, which cost very little money to produce and resulted in high ratings, was quickly followed up with a seemingly endless series of shows subjecting people to competitions, humiliating circumstances, and public criticism by "experts" because . . . well . . . it sells. Love them or hate them, these shows are phenomenal examples of one of the biggest traps out there: seeking fame for fame's sake.

Sadly, in some cases, reality shows have had tragic results, leading to deep depression, suicide, and even murder.

I'll say this once and then I'll get off the soapbox: if it's fame you seek, save yourself time and effort and apply for every reality show you can (they're shockingly easy to get onto), leave your self-respect at the door, get a great therapist, and keep an eye out for your fifteen minutes, because it will go by quickly. Just ask the former casts of any one of these shows . . . if you can remember them!

If, however, it's applause you crave—a genuine celebration of your artistic and public contributions—go forth and conquer! The world will clap when it's earned, and you'll appreciate the difference. The difference is a career.

The "De Niro Effect"

Here's another thing to consider on the topic of fame. I heard this on the radio while driving down Sunset Boulevard a few years back. The DJ was speaking to an author who was writing a piece on celebrity. The author was talking about an interview she had done with Robert De Niro in which she had asked him what was his biggest regret from his career. She said his response was simple (paraphrased from memory here): "Becoming famous too quickly." He claimed that after the movie *Taxi Driver* had shot him into the stratosphere of Hollywood, he immediately stopped receiving constructive criticism from any-one around him. I later found this quote from De Niro that echoes the sentiment: "The hardest thing about being famous is that people are always nice to you. You're in a conversation, and everybody's agreeing with what you're saying—even if you say something totally crazy. You need people who can tell you what you don't want to hear."

According to this interviewer, De Niro went on to say that the effect of all this was to make him increasingly fearful of tak-ing the risks he used to relish, the risks that had defined his act-ing in the first place. He became acutely aware that from that point on he would never be able to fully trust his feedback! Wow! What a scary place to be! The only worse scenario I can think of (and this is also frighteningly common) would be to not recognize this kind of social shift (as De Niro clearly did) and to actually start believing all of the un-vetted praise! Which brings me back to crack cocaine. . . .

Are you lazy?

You need to take a good hard look in the mirror on this one. I personally thank the heavens for all of the ridiculously tal-ented yet lazy people in the world, and so did Mark Twain, who said, "Let us be thankful for the fools; but for them the rest of us could not succeed."

I can say with absolute certainty that the one real advantage I have always had over most of the aspiring artists around me is that I could out-work and out-hustle just about all of them.

I highly recommend seeking out interviews and biographies about Will Smith to see an example of the way drive and work ethic can define a career. In a 2008 exposé on Will Smith on *60 minutes,* the most recurrent characteristic that his friends and family cited was his unparalleled work ethic, whether working on a movie, an album, or even just taking out the

> Let us be thankful for the fools; but for them the rest of us could not succeed.
> —*Mark Twain*

trash. He makes sure he is the best in *everything*, and his approach has definitely paid off.

Herein lies a great opportunity, especially if, like me, you're not the most talented or best trained of the current talent pool. It's an opportunity simply because you have 100 percent control over this variable, and it's something you can do or change about yourself today that will instantly put you ahead of the game, because the truth is, most of your competition is lazy, no matter how talented they are.

Not sure if you're lazy? Ask your friends, family, coworkers, or teachers right now; tell them to be honest, and listen to their responses. Bottom line, if you're not a true go-getter in every sense, this is *not* the right profession for you.

How important is lifestyle to you?

This question addresses your own comfort level, and the answer will be different for everyone because there is an infinite number of variables at play for everyone. Unless you're very well supported financially, be prepared to make sacrifices in both time and in creature comforts.

This industry requires you to maximize your available daylight time for auditions, meetings, networking, classes, and research. Normal jobs simply don't work very well with these requirements, and a lot of "subsistence" night jobs will likely only afford you the basic necessities.

Once you're making money, it's just as critical to know how to invest and protect it for a rainy day!

Working on my first TV series, *2GE+HER*, I made a large pile of money in a very short period of time. Immediately afterward, I lost a sizable chunk of it in the dot-com bust, and after that I went another two years without a decent paying job when several of the entertainment unions went on strike. Unfortunately, the momentum of my success cooled significantly in the meantime.

I never bought that Ferrari, though, and because I maintained the same lifestyle of living below my means, I survived comfortably without having to ever resort to finding a "real job."

At least I survived. Several of my colleagues in entertainment from around the same time who were in similar situations didn't fare so well and had their expensive homes foreclosed on and their BMWs repossessed. That's tough to bounce back from even if you are still the "it" guy or girl!

I'll lay out the basic financial principles that you will need to survive and thrive in this rollercoaster business in chapter 11, Get Rich and Stay Rich: Five Rules to Live By Now.

How well do you handle rejection?

Robert De Niro once said, referring to the start of his acting career:

> I didn't have a problem with rejection, because when you go into an audition, you're rejected already. There are hundreds of other actors. You're behind the eight ball when you go in there.

I love this quote; it clearly demonstrates the difference between how a successful artist thinks, even at the beginning of his career, as compared to most folks who never bothered to prepare themselves. De Niro had truly embraced the fact that most of this industry is a numbers game and *not* personal—as human beings tend to make things.

This one aspect of the industry will weed out most people rather quickly and the majority of others eventually. Some may survive a few digs initially, but if you can't find a way to constructively manage outright and deeply personalized nastiness toward you, this industry will ultimately eat you alive.

It's natural to want to avoid rejection at all costs. Here's my advice: Overcome it, and do it quickly. Don't worry, I'll elaborate on ways to do this later, but know that every single success in this business had to get through some really horrible stories of rejection. Some use it to empower themselves to "get even." After all, as they say, success is the ultimate revenge! And some simply managed to acquire a thick skin and soldier forward, living by the old adage "That which doesn't kill you makes you stronger."

Believe me, I've had some doozies, but you'll have to keep reading to hear them!

Is [acting, singing, dancing, juggling . . . whatever] your "everything"?

This question is a component of desire and what drives you. While anything that gives you a powerful and all-consuming need to succeed can and will act as the backbone for your future triumphs, nothing will keep you more focused on your ultimate goal more than that *desire*—the art itself.

I know several people who are very talented at certain creative arts, but they're no more passionate about it that I am about eating bologna. I don't mind bologna, but I don't dream much about it either. By the same token, I've known very mediocre talents who have excelled to great heights simply because their passion was so deep that they made it happen. Any teenage pop stars come to mind?

Rachael Ray is a tremendous example of someone who did what she loved and that single ingredient became the secret to her success. Rachael's passion has always been food, which took her to New York in 1995, the same year I arrived. Her deep and unwavering passion for cooking was there long before the Food Network looked anything like it looks today. All she knew was that she needed to be around food and share her passion for cooking meals with others.

This passion led her from working the candy counter at the world famous Macy's to managing the fresh foods department there—neither of which would be considered by most to be very glamorous jobs. From there, she went on to become a buyer for Cowan & Lobel, a gourmet food market in Albany, New York, in part to be closer to her family and where she grew up (family is also a passion for Rachael).

Back home, she began teaching a class—often for free—called "30-Minute Meals," inspired by customers she met at the store who seemed to be somewhat cooking-averse. This class led to a weekly spot on the Schenectady station WRGB, a book called *30-Minute Meals,* and then her first Food Network contract in 2001, only six years later!

Only four years after that, Rachael Ray was courted by the queen of talk TV, Oprah Winfrey, to host the record-breaking series, *Rachael Ray,* and the rest, as they say, is history.

One of the biggest assets that will help you get through the rejection, the exhaustion of eighteen hour days, the sleepless nights, the agonizing self-doubts, and all the rest of it will be that unbridled drive to do what you love more than anything else in life. But you need to be somewhat realistic about answering the next question first. . . .

Are you any good?

Few things are more painful than watching someone who is clearly passionate about their art try to perform when they are, by all commercial standards, awful. You certainly don't need to watch *American Idol* (or any other talent competition show) very long to see just how many misguided people there are out there . . . and to see those people humiliated by the panel of so-called experts on national television.

Reality show politics aside, the fact is that as a performer you are entering a business in which you hope that people will one day *pay you* to entertain them. Even if your mother, your family, your spouse, or your friends' love runs so deep that they're blind to your inabilities, the rest of the world won't be, and most won't want to give you money to see you flail pathetically.

I hope that by now you have some awareness of where you stand in terms of ability. In all probability, if you do have something creative to offer commercially, you've already been told as much by lots of people: "Hey you'd be amazing on stage, film,

TV, radio, print, in commercials, etc. . . ." If that hasn't happened to you by now, take a good hard look at why you're considering this life for yourself.

If any of the above questions raised red flags in your head, congratulations! You have the last question nailed:

Can you be honest with yourself?

If you are, then you are in a position to effect change to any of the shortcomings mentioned above using information you'll find in the following pages.

If the above questions only served to reinforce your confidence in going forward, then you're already ahead of the pack and ready to get out there.

Rule 2: Determine honestly if this business is for you.

PART II

THINK

The one and only thing that we as human beings have 100 percent control over in our lives, regardless of the situation, is how we think in any given moment. Whether it's our approach to something, our reaction to something, or what we choose to focus our thoughts on, the most powerful tool we all have at our disposal is the tool of consciously using our thoughts to our best advantage.

There is no better example of this truth in my opinion than Viktor Frankl's account of being a concentration camp survivor in Germany during World War II, presented in his book *Man's Search for Meaning.* In an unimaginable environment entirely dictated by ruthless guards, where decisions over life and death were being made with no provocation, and having been robbed of all measure of personal property and basic respect as a fellow human being, Viktor Frankl discovered that the key to a meaningful human existence was in choosing to maintain control over one's own thoughts.

Since we are all, to some degree, products of our unique environments and personal history, some folks have just had the advantage of having been taught successful ways of thinking while others have not been so lucky. Viktor Frankl, for example, was a psychiatrist and neurologist by trade, and he spent his life in search of useful and advantageous ways of thinking.

Wherever you are now in that spectrum, however, at this moment in time you have the choice and opportunity to adopt ways of thinking that successful people have used throughout history to acquire everything they have ever dreamed of.

Training your mind to think for success is not just about having a positive mental attitude (or PMA, as you may have heard it called) though that helps; it's about choosing your thoughts consciously, wisely, and effectively. By default, most people let their thoughts "just happen," and for most people, their thoughts are almost always dictated by their upbringing, which in turn creates mental and emotional habits. This is all well and good if you were raised in an environment of successful people who taught successful thinking patterns to you.

Most of us though, regardless of upbringing, could use some fine-tuning at the very least—some people could use a full mental overhaul. Luckily, the basics of successful thinking are indeed basic, and with nothing more than persistence, you'll find them easy to adopt. Why? Because it'll just *feel right.* It will probably just make a lot more sense than what you've been doing habitually all along, and you'll probably notice it working to your advantage almost immediately. So get ready to change your mind and change your life!

Change Your Mind—Change Your Life

Researchers at the University of Mississippi conducted a study to discover why people fail. In over 90 percent of the cases they examined, a person's chosen behavior—a reflection of their thinking—caused their failure. Simply stated, most people have the skills, knowledge, experience, and education to succeed. In the cases where they fail, they simply lack the personal belief that they're capable of success.

—Robert Kiyosaki (Rich Dad Coaching Online)

This is a very powerful concept. Remember the one overall theorem for this book that I mentioned earlier?

Successful people *think* differently than unsuccessful people.

So how *do* successful artists think? What key features define the mindset that paves their road to success? *The Big Three of Successful Thinking,* as I like to call them, are the foundations that I believe you must have in order to build any significant career in entertainment: *belief, vision,* and *standards.*

I promise you that if you fully commit to making the changes necessary to adopt these three foundations, it will not only bring to your doorstep all of the entertainment opportunities you desire, but it will also change your life.

Belief

I have never in my entire career met a successful artist who said that they truly never believed that they would succeed. Many had doubts along the way, sure, but they all believed, even if it was little more than a suspicion, that they would get to where they are today—myself included.

> Doing the unrealistic is easier than doing the realistic.
>
> —*Tim Ferris*

I'm now about to pose one of the most important questions to you that will determine whether or not you will achieve your dreams:

Do you believe you will succeed?

You'll notice I didn't ask: Do you believe you *might* succeed? Or: Do you believe it's *possible* to succeed? Or even: What do you think are the odds that you might succeed? In fact, the words we use to communicate with ourselves and others make a critical distinction for success that absolutely needs to be made, but before I go there—and I will in a later chapter—take note of the first reaction that came to mind when you read the words above.

Did you immediately react with a yes? Did you sheepishly pause, thinking of what you *should* say but feeling something less adamant? Did you—gasp—say no? However you reacted, make a quick note of it and keep reading; and remember, we're being honest here!

Tim Ferris, in his book *The 4-Hour Workweek,* makes a valid argument, one that I wholeheartedly subscribe to:

> It's lonely at the top. Ninety-nine percent of people in the world are convinced they are incapable of achieving

great things, so they aim for mediocre. The level of competition is thus fiercest for "realistic" goals, paradoxically making them the most time and energy-consuming. It is easier to raise $10,000,000 than it is to raise $1,000,000.

If you are insecure, guess what? The rest of the world is too. Do not overestimate the competition and underestimate yourself. You are better than you think.

So, there goes the most common excuse for not believing your dreams are obtainable—because everyone else thinks so too!

The power of the ability to believe goes far beyond solid rational thinking, and here are three reasons, from my own experience, why I personally feel that the ability to believe is among the most critical components to determining whether or not you will see your name in lights or succeed beyond your wildest imagination in any avenue you pursue.

1. My Own Experience

I will never forget the moment, at six years of age, when I was playing in the living room of our house in Baltimore, Maryland, and all of a sudden, I *knew* that I was going to be on television one day. In fact, so real was the notion, the calling, the daydream (whatever you want to call it), that I felt the need to start preparing for interviews immediately—the kind of interviews Ed McMahon would conduct with a contestant after a winning performance on *Star Search,* for example (*Star Search* was big at the time).

What set this experience apart from any other of the many daydreams I'd had was the complete matter-of-fact certainty with which I *knew* my destiny and, perhaps more telling, the sudden responsibility I felt that came with knowing ahead of time what was coming.

From that day on (until now, of course), I never spoke of this experience. I kept it as my little secret. I often fell back on it when I felt obsolete, overlooked, or discouraged. At those moments I simply reminded myself that these experiences were merely the dues I had to pay, because after all, even though I knew my destiny was a given, I had to have a good story to tell Ed!

I'm willing to bet that you too, at some point, have had a glimpse at the great "you" you would be someday. Did you listen?

2. Case Studies

I have pored over hundreds of interviews, autobiographies, and biographies of extremely successful artists, and I have noticed that the experience mentioned above was a common theme with nearly all of them.

The way in which the person came to believe in their future success or destiny varied from person to person, of course. Some seemed to be born with the notion, some had encouraging parents, others had an epiphany at some point in time or experienced a life-changing event that triggered it. Still others had no other choice but to survive, or they may have learned to believe by doing what I have learned to do in later years with a technique I'll spell out for you later.

Regardless of their personal experience, however, all of these successful people believed in their hearts that they would eventually succeed at achieving their goal. Here are some quotes from a few very well-known achievers who are (or were) also adamant believers:

> The thing always happens that you really believe in; and the belief in a thing makes it happen.
>
> —FRANK LLOYD WRIGHT, ARCHITECT

> Back of every creation, supporting it like an arch, is faith. Enthusiasm is nothing: it comes and goes. But if one believes, then miracles occur.
>
> —HENRY MILLER, AUTHOR AND LITERARY INNOVATOR

Believe and act as if it were impossible to fail.

—CHARLES F. KETTERING, INVENTOR OF THE ELECTRIC STARTER

3. Science

A litany of scientific, psychological, sociological, and human behavioral studies cite the ability to believe and the notion of faith as among the strongest determining variables in whether or not a single person—even a driven person—will, in fact, succeed.

From these references and exhaustive double blind studies, we've all learned such terms as *Pygmalion effect* and *placebo effect* and the concept of the *self-fulfilling prophecy.* Time and again, science proves that if you can convince someone to believe a thing is true, they will reliably manifest the expected result.

In studies that demonstrate the Pygmalion effect, students who were generally thought to be poor performers and incapable of stronger work (often with diagnosed learning disabilities) were transformed into high achievers simply by moving them to new schools and telling the new teachers that they were, in fact, gifted high achievers.

Because the new teachers believed them to be gifted students, they treated the students as such, and the students in turn fulfilled the high expectations placed on them and flourished as a result.

Many studies have shown that when subjects are given a placebo (also known as a sugar pill) and told that it is a powerful medication, their bodies literally generate on their own the required chemicals to treat the disorder.

The exciting thing about science that supports belief and faith is the idea that if you can be tricked into belief and faith, then you can learn to harness it, and therefore it can be used as a tool for personal achievement.

Acquiring and Strengthening Belief

Think about your immediate response to the question *Do you believe you will succeed?* This will give you an idea of how far you have to go to obtain the power of belief.

If your answer to the question was an immediate Yes, then you are likely already using a form of the technique I'm about to describe, and you will likely benefit from a structured way to increase its effectiveness.

The more hesitation between an immediate Yes all the way down to the kiss of death: "No, I don't believe I will succeed," the more you will have to work hard to create the habits necessary to acquire the tool of belief.

The good news is that it does not have to be something you were born with. It is something that you can systematically train into yourself. It does, however, require a little work, a lot of repetition, and at least a little blind faith from the outset.

Because our conscious human "software" tends to demand proof first before believing anything, the technique I am going to share with you systematically targets the impressionable subconscious, which has the power to *create* proof for our critical conscious mind.

Autosuggestion

The basic technique of accessing the power of belief is a process often referred to as autosuggestion or autogenic training, whereby you systematically train the subconscious mind to believe something without immediate proof. This simple yet effective technique is based on the practice of visualization combined with emotion and repetition.

This quick and easy-to-implement tool requires a little blind faith, but let me assure you, the results will amaze you.

The autosuggestion technique that follows is the process I have used for as long as I can remember and was taught to me by my mother who was a practicing clinical psychologist through out most of my childhood. Similar versions are taught by any number of credible teachers.

1. Write down exactly what it is that you would like to achieve in an absolute tense. For example: "I *will* star in a major motion picture."
2. Add to the statement an exact time frame. For example: "I will star in a major motion picture *within three years.*"
3. At minimum, every evening before bed and every morning when you wake up, read or recite the statement and then visualize it actually taking place in as much detail as your wild imagination can muster. Make especially certain to enjoy the powerful emotions that realizing this dream invokes.

The measurable success of this basic technique has been documented in many studies, including in several noteworthy experiments conducted by French psychologist Émile Coué and German psychiatrist Johannes Schultz. Its effectiveness, according to their numerous clinical trials, correlates directly to the quality of visualization, the level of emotion attached to the visualization, and the amount of repetition. In other words, more is better! The goal of this practice is to subconsciously train (or "trick," if you will) the conscious mind into accepting, as fact, a certain premise; in this case the premise that you will, without question, achieve your dream(s).

Vision

> Don't be afraid of the space between your dreams and reality. If you can dream it, you can make it so.
>
> —BELVA DAVIS, VICE PRESIDENT OF A.F.T.R.A. AND RECIPIENT OF THE
> NATIONAL ACADEMY OF TELEVISION ARTS AND SCIENCES' HIGHEST
> LIFETIME ACHIEVEMENT AWARD, THE GOVERNOR'S AWARD

What does your dream look like? When you arrive, who will be there around you? Where will you be? What are the sounds? The smells? How will it feel?

The second foundation for successful thinking is having a

clear and specific vision of what it is you desire. This third step in autogenic training is simple and very powerful.

Being able to clearly and passionately articulate a vision is such a powerful tool, in fact, that tapping into this power has become a hot topic in recent years. One example of this is the best-selling book and movie, *The Secret,* which purports to teach a practical method for obtaining our desires through a practice of visualization that taps into what the author, Rhonda Byrne, calls "the law of attraction."

This is one area I'm not going to even try and sell you: the how or why visualization works. I just know that, in my experience, it does. I'm not really interested in knowing exactly how a microwave works either: I just want my coffee heated quickly, so I push the button that says *Start.* I have found some things that help a great deal in taking advantage of this tool, however.

The main difference between a successful artist's and a non-successful artist's visions are that the successful artist actively creates and nurtures his or her vision with detailed visualization, repetition, and emotion, while the non-successful artist has only a wishy-washy, vague, and passive notion of what his or her dream really is.

In fact, I can describe for you several specific visions I've had, created, and nurtured over the course of my career, and not only did all of them come true, but they often did so in frighteningly accurate detail.

My six-year-old self envisioned being driven into Times Square in a black stretch limo with a white interior and walking out into throngs of screaming fans as I walked the red carpet into my first movie premiere. I visualized myself wearing leather pants (like the rock stars I worshiped), I saw the photographers' faces, smelled popcorn, and I even remembered the temporary metal barricade that kept the people off the carpet. I'll never forget the moment in 1998 when I arrived at the premiere for my first starring role in a film, *2GE+HER*—the door to the limo opened and I saw the unusual white interior. Next we were dropped off right in the heart of Times Square.

A freaky, surreal, and poignant feeling came over me as I experienced the exact moment I had envisioned, exactly how I had pictured it a million times before in my head: limo interior, location, clothes, marquee, popcorn, barricade, and all.

When I had envisioned the day I would perform on stage as a rock star, I always pictured a large outdoor stadium on the water for some reason (I was a Yankees fan). In 1997, I was asked to join Russia's hottest band of the day, Ha-Ha, and I was promptly flown out to Moscow to record and tour with them. Within two weeks of landing in Russia, I found myself performing on stage in front of more than thirty thousand people in Yalta's largest outdoor concert arena, which overlooks the Black Sea. And yes, for a guy who two weeks ago had been bartending for rent money, it was just as mind-blowing as it sounds. Not too many years later with the film, series, and band *2GE+HER*, I found myself back on stage at the Jones Beach Amphitheater, packed with more than twenty thousand fans, overlooking the water, as we headlined a radio tour concert.

By the time 2GE+HER was opening up for Brittney Spears in 2000, I had played so many arenas and stadiums that I no longer needed that dream or vision.

I've heard countless stories like mine over the years about dreams coming true exactly how a person had visualized it, but none compare to the story my good friend Nigel Dick, perhaps the most celebrated and prolific music video director of all time, relayed to me.

Nigel was part of the movement that literally started the music video genre as we know it. He has directed the vast majority of the most celebrated music videos ever produced, and by far the most videos overall. He is often credited with giving big bands their big break into superstardom as a result of his work; bands like Guns N' Roses and Def Leppard, for example.

Nigel was hired to direct the movie *2GE+HER*. One night we

were talking about how some of our dreams had come true and the freaky circumstances under which they came to fruition.

Nigel told me that when he was a kid he wanted to be Jimmy Page, the famed guitarist for Led Zeppelin. He explained to me that he didn't want to be *like* Jimmy Page, he literally wanted to be Jimmy Page, and he spent his entire childhood visualizing what that would be like.

Nigel went on to become an architect and later realized that he needed to pursue his true passion: music. When he changed careers, he found himself on the cusp of the burgeoning music video industry. (You know—the one that killed the radio star?) Several years later, he had become one of the most sought-after music video directors in the world. When an opportunity to produce Robert Plant's first solo video came up, he immediately seized it. The following description is from his website and is the short version of the story he relayed to me.

> I was producing Robert Plant's first ever solo video, which Robbo directed. His guitar player didn't show up, so I got to be his stand-in. For a moment I thought: "If that's Robert Plant over there—then I must be Jimmy Page!" I'd always dreamed of somehow being Jimmy Page, which is why I had that cheesy Les Paul copy. Moral: Be careful what you wish for—it often comes true but not in the way you'd imagined.

Now if *that's* possible, then your goals are too! As Nigel's story points out, it may not always manifest itself exactly the way we pictured it, but it almost never fails to disappoint!

Once again, the logical question is *How does this work?* And the truth is, no one really knows for sure. Many people, like Nigel and me, just know that it does. The useful question however, is *How do I make it work for me?*

There are countless advisors, coaches, and teachers out there willing to teach or sell you their method and philosophy for manifesting your dreams. A few books that have influenced me in particular and that I believe are well worth exploring are (in no particular order):

- Deepak Chopra's *The Seven Spiritual Laws of Success*
- Dr. Wayne Dyer's *Manifest Your Destiny*
- Napoleon Hill's *Think and Grow Rich*
- Uell S. Andersen's *Three Magic Words*
- Anthony Robbins's *Personal Power*
- Rhonda Byrne's *The Secret*

Is one better than the other? Probably not, as long as it works for you.

It has actually been shown with the use of MRIs that our brains cannot distinguish the difference between something that has taken place in real life and a visualization of something taking place, provided that a high commitment to that visualization exists.

In fact, this is the very same basic technique that many sports psychologists have been using to cure professional athletes from their slumps. They coach the athlete to repeatedly visualize the perfect game while attaching emotions to the positive outcome, and the results have been powerful enough to create a very lucrative cottage industry of professional sports psychology!

Standards

> Good ideas are not adopted automatically. They must be driven into practice with courageous patience.
> —HYMAN RICKOVER, THE "FATHER OF THE NUCLEAR NAVY"

One truth that has stuck with me from my childhood comes from my dad. Dad never lost an opportunity to point out the standards the greatest achievers in our society held themselves to. He would regale me with stories of how the greatest tennis players of the day, like John McEnroe or Bjorn Borg, would practice a specific shot for ten or more hours a day; how Pelé, the most famous soccer player in history, would juggle a grapefruit around the house with his feet when he wasn't practicing on the field; and how Michael Jordan would stay on the court late into the night, long after his teammates left practice.

After leaving the army, my father quickly became one of the most respected doctors in his field, even writing several of the textbooks required for becoming a dermatologist today. This never surprised me for a second as I watched my dad work just as hard at his profession as I imagine Michael Jordan, John McEnroe, Bjorn Borg, or Pelé did at their sports.

As a child, inspired by his early advice, I distinctly remember hitting tennis balls against the wall for five or six hours a day in the basement at an early age . . . and I didn't even really love tennis all that much! I just loved Dad's stories, because although I wasn't naturally good at a lot of things, I knew that holding myself to a higher standard than most people would give me a distinct advantage.

Before long I could play with and beat many kids twice my age. I didn't continue to play much tennis after that—as I said, I didn't really love it—but what I did love was the power that this newfound knowledge gave me! My new secret worked, and it worked really well.

It all boils down to standards and what we expect out of ourselves. I can assure you that if you want to be a successful, working entertainer, then you need to start having higher standards for yourself than anyone around you, and higher than anyone else expects out of you.

If most people you know think practicing an instrument for three hours a day is a lot, then practice ten. Both Keith Urban and Brad Paisley, for example, have told me they still practice an obscene amount by most standards; and they're widely considered to be two of the best guitar players in country music already.

If fellow acting students memorize and rehearse one monologue a week, then do fifteen. If the folks waiting tables along-side you go to two auditions a week, then make the decision to go to two a *day.*

Whatever it is, make sure your personal standards are higher than anyone else's. If the examples above seem way overboard, you're right, they are . . . by most standards. In reality, however, these examples are probably not overboard *enough.*

You really, truly need to be obscene about this, and if you are, you will automatically place yourself in the top 1 percent of the entertainment industry. And it's the top 1 percent that gets all the rewards, all the jobs, all the money, and all the praise.

Throughout my career and after studying the most success-ful people in this industry, I have learned that this is one piece of the pie you cannot skip. Everybody you can think of, at this moment, who has succeeded enough to be considered a super-star, has held themselves to obscenely high standards by most normal definitions.

It may take a while to build your standards, but if you begin slowly you will quickly find that your comfort zone for doing and expecting more from yourself will grow tremendously in a pretty short period of time. The key is to stretch a little bit each time!

In the fantastic book *Outliers,* author Malcolm Gladwell coins the phrase "the 10,000-hour rule," which demonstrates that the über-successful people in history, people he calls out-liers, such as Bill Gates, Mozart, the Beatles, and Michael Jor-dan, all put in no fewer than ten thousand dedicated and focused hours toward their discipline. Consider this excerpt from the book, which cites a very interesting study:

> The striking thing about Ericsson's study is that he and his colleagues couldn't find any "naturals," musicians who floated effortlessly to the top while practicing a fraction of the time their peers did. Nor could they find any "grinds," people who worked harder than everyone

else, yet just didn't have what it takes to break top ranks. Their research suggests that once a musician has enough ability to get into a top music school, the thing that distinguishes one performer from another is how hard he or she works. That's it. And what's more, the people at the very top don't work just harder or even much harder than everyone else. They work much, much harder. . . .

"The emerging picture from such studies is that ten thousand hours of practice is required to achieve the level of mastery associated with being a world-class expert in anything," writes the neurologist Daniel Levitin. "In study after study, of composers, basketball players, fiction writers, ice skaters, concert pianists, chess players, master criminals, and what have you, this number [ten thousand] comes up again and again. (*Outliers,* p. 31)

Gladwell goes on to lay out some pretty solid theories as to why this is, but the simple fact is that you can't get around putting in the time, and you can't avoid having much, much higher standards than the average Joe if you want to succeed in this business.

Perhaps therein lies the main reason that so many of the popular competition-based reality-show participants, winners or losers, have such a difficult time finding any meaningful success, despite their obvious natural talents. They just haven't put in ten thousand hours yet, and their standards for themselves simply aren't high enough.

Rule 3: Fully commit to believing in your success, to the specific vision of that dream materializing, and to raising your standards exponentially higher than they are now.

Perspective Is Everything

Most often it's the way you see a problem that is the problem.

—PROVERB

One of the fascinating things I've noticed when reading autobiographies of successful artists is that they all tend to see life from a similar perspective. And over and over again I've found two distinct qualities among some of the most successful entertainers that make up the foundation of a successful perspective: *optimism* and *focus.* In the simplest terms, they see life and their dreams as a bunch of possibilities and opportunities, and they know what to focus on in any given situation to make sure they realize those dreams.

Optimism: More Than Just "Glass Half Full"

The Six-Pack

Optimism in the eyes of a successful artist requires at least six critical assumptions:

1. Anything is possible.

2. There is almost always more than one solution to a problem.
3. There's almost always a better solution than the most commonly held view.
4. You always have control over a successful outcome.
5. There is no such thing as failure, only other options and opportunities.
6. Life is boundless.

Think about it for a second: if Oprah Winfrey didn't have the perspective that anything was possible, do you really think she would have bothered trying to break into a predominantly male, all-white, looks-obsessed industry like television news in 1973? What she ultimately accomplished had never been done before, but that didn't stop her.

Not only that, but she had to circumnavigate many monumental obstacles en route to success; obstacles (just a few of them mentioned already) that most typical people would think insurmountable.

She believed she could control her outcome, and by harnessing that belief she created huge opportunities for herself and, through the *Oprah* show, huge opportunities for others like Dr. Phil and Dr. Oz; not to mention the positive legacy for her viewers who have become inspired to read through her book club, or inspired by guests with tremendous success stories.

Oprah's empire, one that includes magazines, several dozen companies, and even her own TV network, clearly demonstrates that she views life and her future with perhaps the purest sense of boundlessness ever displayed in the media to date.

Fully embrace those six assumptions, and you will begin to exponentially improve your odds for success in the entertainment industry immediately!

Or how about this: every single world record ever achieved happened because someone was optimistic that the ultimate line had not been drawn yet. The four-minute mile was unheard of until Roger Bannister broke it in 1954 with a time of 3:59.4.

Before that it was absolutely unthinkable. Now there are people, regular people, doing it everyday! That's perspective at work. Remember Henry Ford's sage words "Whether you think you can or think you can't—you are right!"

Think you're not a good enough singer to perform with Carrie Underwood? A good enough actor to work alongside Ryan Gosling? Are you going to let that stop you? Would Oprah have? Or Roger Bannister? Or Henry Ford?

Perhaps the most critical difference between truly successfully optimistic people and those that aren't is in whether their optimism is passive or not. Remember assumption 4: You always have control over a successful outcome.

This is the difference between: "I'm optimistic that it will all work out" versus "I'm optimistic that *I can make this* work out." One is passive, and the other demonstrates that you are in control of the situation.

Courtesy of Peter H. Thomas, in his book *Be Great,* here are a few other artists who took control of their situations and made things work out, despite searing rejections, setbacks, and seemingly impossible odds:

- Barbara Walters was told by Don Hewitt, who later became the producer of *60 Minutes,* to "stay out of television." She became one of the most famous women in TV anyway.

- Steven Spielberg's mediocre grades meant he could not get into UCLA's film school. He made *ET* and *Close Encounters* anyway.

- John Grisham's first novel, *A Time To Kill,* was rejected by sixteen agents and twelve publishers. He became a bestselling author anyway.

- The Beatles were rejected by Decca Records in 1962. They became the world's most famous rock band anyway.

- Elvis Presley's music teacher in Memphis told him he couldn't carry a tune. He became "the King" anyway.

- Billy Crystal was chosen as an original cast member for *Sat-*

urday Night Live but was cut from the cast before the first show aired. He went on to star in highly successful comedies anyway. (*Be Great,* p. 170)

The single most important word in this list, in my opinion, comes at the very end of each item and represents the spirit and power of optimism. That word is *anyway.*

Assuming that by now you've probably embraced the reality that you will become the successful performer you envision . . . anyway, and you are beginning to act on these new standards, which are significantly higher than those of your competition . . . anyway, you now have to face the day-to-day realities of making it happen. This is where most people get tripped up. After all, it's the little obstacles we come across that too often make us want to revert back to old excuses and become cynics!

> Cynics put their finger on the disease before they put it on health. It's the easy way to go. Play the blame game: "I got screwed, that should've been mine." They're all dead-end answers.
>
> —Matthew McConaughey

Achievers, however, never lose sight of the bigger picture, and they refuse to make excuses or get bogged down in small details. This is a crucial difference in perspective.

On Getting an Agent

Consider, for example, the challenge of getting a top tier agent, whether for acting, music, modeling, writing, directing, whatever. Agents are generally—and somewhat accurately—considered to be a necessary tool in getting a big break or at least that first break.

Many people have discovered that this challenge is something of a Catch-22, however—you can't get access to good job opportunities without an agent, but you can't get an agent without having proven yourself in a good job. And if that's how you view it, it's certainly true!

Just say out loud that you're looking for an agent in LA or New York, and you'll hear variations on the same basic advice, frequently offered by agents themselves: Step One: Get into some kind of working production, and Step Two: Invite agents to come see you. All you need to do then is hope they show up and pray you wow them more than the other performers next to you do.

In other words: don't go to them, they'll find you!

With this perspective, your only hope is to step out into the vast sea of fellow dreamers (all of your possible competition— precisely the competition you hope to eliminate by being represented by a top agent) and then hope and pray you'll be the one to get snatched up at a showcase, one of hundreds you may have to do to be seen by a reputable agent.

And let's face it: what are the odds that your performance in anything obscure on one particular night is going to be so phenomenal that William Morris is going to decide to risk their reputation on signing you—an unknown? I'm sure it happens, but in my experience, considering I was just starting out at age twenty-three after going to college to study business consulting, I didn't like those odds. The process, to me, sounded like it would at best take a while—at worst, forever!

I refused to buy into the unhelpful perspective/myth that this industry is a competition designed to weed out the least talented, the not-so-attractive, and the not-connected. I chose to believe that it is merely designed to weed out the shortsighted, the uncreative, and the quitters. Talent, I was certain, had little to do with it.

A Winning Perspective

Most of the folks I met when I first arrived in New York were trying to be seen by top agents as I described, but I referred to numbers two and three in the list of positive assumptions above and remembered that there are always many more, and often much better, solutions to a challenge.

So I asked the question: How many other ways are there to get an agent—that most other people won't do or won't think to do?

When I first arrived in New York City in the winter of 1995, I kept hearing these rules about what you should *never ever* do regarding agents: *Never* cold-call agencies on the phone and *never ever . . . ever* go into an agency without an appointment! And—you guessed it—it's not gonna be easy to get an appointment! That's one hell of a filter; I figured some folks must have slipped through it and I planned on slipping through as well.

The good news about all of this is that because of this filter, most aspiring talent do not have agents, which means that if you choose to find a faster and more reliable way to go about acquiring an agent, you're leaving most of your peers behind to flounder, wallow, complain, and quit—usually in that order. Perspective! Remember Tim Ferris's winning perspective? "Doing the unrealistic is easier than doing the realistic. . . . The competition is always fiercest at the middle!"

So here's exactly what I did: The first part of my agent-acquiring strategy was influenced by the book *How to Win Friends and Influence People* by Dale Carnegie, written in 1936 and still the best book of its kind in print today, in my opinion.

Carnegie's Principle #5: "Talk in terms of the other person's interests."

I first tried to put myself in the agent's shoes. My goal was to systematically provide him or her with what *I would want* to be provided with if I were the agent considering a new client. And no, it's not gifts, by the way!

I figured out rather quickly that an agent's bottom line is finding and cultivating a moneymaking artist, period. Remember the 90/10 rule? It's 90 percent business after all!

I further surmised that agents would be looking for proof that you can make them money and proof that you'll be marketable for a while down the road.

After asking around, I found that these moneymaking qualities fit into industry categories, and I figured it would benefit me to define myself—for them—using those categories: commercial, theatrical, TV, film, radio, comedic, dramatic, character, leading man, musician.

Even though I considered myself capable of fitting into several categories, I figured *commercial* sounded the most "money," so I went with that simply because the money stream in entertainment always starts with advertising.

Next, I took stock of what I already had to prove I could be a money generator, and I set about filling in the gaps. One thing I had going for me was a few commercials I had done in New Orleans, a much easier market than LA, New York, or Chicago to get first-time work. I edited the commercials together in a way that made me appear to be the main focus of each, rationalizing that, after all, what would be the odds that they would have seen my local commercial in New Orleans, right?

One down—I'm now *commercial*.

The other tangible asset I had was the one modeling job I did in New Orleans, which happened to be a billboard for New Orleans Original Daiquiris, so I had a friend who was still living in New Orleans take a picture of the billboard, which still sat high above Canal Street. Then I printed a bunch of eight-by-ten copies of the picture.

I still figured that wasn't quite enough, so next I went to NYU's photography department and found an eager student who was willing to do a photo shoot for me in exchange for the practice and to build his portfolio, and we set out to replicate a real clothing ad in a well-known Italian fashion magazine that I had found in a bookstore.

With that picture, I went to Kinko's and literally created a fake "tear-sheet" (an industry term describing modeling work torn from the magazine you were featured in), which, remarkably, looked 100 percent legit.

I figured two commercial pictures were enough to convey

my money-making abilities in modeling, and I would simply explain the lack of more pictures in my portfolio by explaining that I had just used modeling to pay the bills while I concentrated on my first passion, acting, which, according to my well-rehearsed pitch, is where my new career focus and a talent agent came in.

In reality, I was such an unlikely model it was laughable, but I planned to present it with such matter-of-factness that I hoped by the time they questioned its plausibility we would be well onto discussing my future career as an actor.

Like many aspiring professional actors, I had done quite a bit of regional theatre during college, so I created a résumé (in the industry standard format at that time) listing my former shows and roles, even including a few of my professors' names under the "Training" section. I was now officially armed with tangible proof that I was a commercial money-maker who had a bit of experience.

Now I needed to work on a sales pitch for myself that would play into their desires. I decided to position myself as a "naive kid" who had stumbled onto a money-generating gift but didn't quite realize it yet. In other words I wanted to create for them an agent's dream. I wanted to let them think that *they* were discovering the next big thing. This, incidentally, is an example of using Dale Carnegie's Principle #7: "Let the other person feel that the idea is his or hers."

My well-crafted innocence, I figured, would appeal to the "We have to grab this kid before someone else does" aspect of human nature (playing to *their* instincts), while at the same time downplaying any holes in my professional entertainment background.

Another thing I had going for me was that at age twenty-three I still convincingly looked sixteen, making me appeal to the long-term money-generating career I thought they would certainly be looking for. (Looking extremely young for my age, if anything, may be my only true natural God-given asset.) So now all I needed was to get in the door to be discovered . . . by design of course!

Getting in the Door

I also assumed, and have since long confirmed, that because agents have made it clear that they do not want to be solicited by artists—even though they always need new blood—they must have a reliable pipeline for new talent of some sort that was more efficient that the traditional scouting method. I didn't really know what this pipeline was, but my instinct told me that it was likely the same as it is for any business: the age-old personal recommendation. I'll cover the importance and skills of networking later on, and as you'll see, this is one of the critical keys to my strategy.

My next logical step was to figure out how to be "that guy," the one who gets recommended. The first several weeks turned up few viable links, but after focusing solely on this one objective obsessively for a few months, I found myself eating lunch at a restaurant that I couldn't afford with an old friend I hadn't seen in years who had lived in New York City his whole life.

It was my hope that after living in New York for thirty-plus years he would know at least *someone* who worked at an agency, and after catching up (he was a former camp counselor of mine), I laid it out. And voilà! It turned out that he did have a friend who worked at an top talent agency in town, though he wasn't 100 percent sure what he did there. Didn't matter to me—I had my in.

The next day, armed with an address, a name, and my "commercial kit"—and praying that my friend had made the call he said he would to introduce me—I did exactly what you're *not* supposed to do: I just showed up. I sat in the waiting room just outside the door to the office that held the nameplate of my friend's friend for about an hour, not realizing that he was actually on vacation. Incidentally, to this day I don't know whether or not my friend actually made the call.

Eventually another door opened and a woman walked out, noticed me, and asked whom I was there to see. When I told her, she told me he was on vacation. Then I quickly pretended I had the wrong date and added that I had to leave town soon for a job (a money-making job), but that I guessed I'd come back again later.

Long story short: she invited me into her office. I showed her my "kit" with all the innocence I could feign, and within two hours she had introduced me to the "commercial" department and . . . I had an agent!

In the end, I got an agent because I *was* a good actor, in the sense that I was able to convince them that I was an ideal candidate for representation. Heck, in hindsight, even *they* couldn't fault me in terms of performance!

Furthermore, the simple fact that they would never expect anyone to just show up worked in my favor, giving me automatic credibility. After all, no one would be that crazy! Everyone knows to *never do that!* (I hear agents cringing all over the world right now.)

Would I do it that way today? Actually, no, but not for the obvious reasons: for one thing, the industry and world have changed significantly since then (like post-9/11 building security for example). Now you really do need an appointment just to get through the front door. Never mind the fact that, having written about it, I just put every single agent on alert, blowing any chance of it working again. But the approach to problem solving would be the same, which in a nutshell is:

1. Figure out the agent's needs/perspective
2. Cater directly to it
3. Focus your attention on becoming "that guy" who gets the personal recommendation

My perspective would also be the same: that there must be a better, quicker, and far more effective way of procuring an agent than setting up a few hundred actor's showcases.

I had been in New York for less than three months and had representation from one of the top agencies in the industry, and it all came down to perspective: Where others saw a problem, I saw opportunities. This story also illustrates a couple of other key skills and traits: focus, creative problem solving, initiative, and instinct.

Focus

Focus is also the second foundation of what makes for a winning perspective. Every step of the way toward acquiring an agent, I had to choose what to focus on and what not to focus on. This was a direct result of the questions I chose to ask, because ultimately it's the questions we ask that control focus.

I could have easily focused on the "rules" about approaching an agent, but instead I asked myself, How can I get around them? I could easily have focused on my lack of any real experience, but instead I asked myself, How can I create the ideal first impression and become someone they *need* in order to make more money easily?

Heck, I could have focused on the fact that I was completely out of money and starving, but instead I asked myself, What will be the long-term effects of having an agent, and are they worth the sacrifice?

The moral: if you focus on problems, you will create more problems. If you focus on creative solutions by asking the right questions, you create solutions, opportunities, and success.

Ultimately there are two components to becoming a master of focus and letting it take you to the top, fast: emotions and magnification. To manage them, you need to understand them.

Emotions

Learning how to utilize focus instead of letting it control you is a very difficult task for many people, because too often our focus is controlled by our emotions. It's far too easy to let our negative emotions, directed by insecurity, dominate our focus.

One of the ways this happens is when we focus way too much of our attention on what we think other people may think about us. And even in the world of entertainment, a career in which our job is to be liked, this is still a *total* waste of time.

> **Dr. Daniel Amen's 18/40/60 Rule:** When you're 18, you worry about what everybody is thinking of you; when you're 40, you don't give a darn about what anybody thinks of you; when you're 60, you realize nobody's been thinking about you at all.
>
> Surprise, surprise! Most of the time, nobody's thinking about you at all! They are too busy worrying about their own lives, and if they are thinking about you at all, they are wondering what you are thinking about them. (Cited in *The Success Principles* by Jack Canfield, p. 45)

The head of one of the biggest film casting agencies in the business once told me something that I never forgot: "Bad auditions don't matter to anyone else but you! Only good auditions matter. It's a numbers game. We [casting directors] simply see way too many people everyday to remember your lackluster performance any more than a few days, but knock our socks off and we see dollar signs. And dollar signs are a casting director's biggest motivation." This applies to any of the creative arts!

Casting directors are under tremendous pressure to perform for their employers. They have far more important things to concentrate on than your bad audition. Besides, any reputable casting director (the only ones you should really care about anyway) knows that every artist has bad days too.

Robert, my long-time agent and friend, has always said: "You are far more likely to be rejected based on your hair color, eye color, skin color, height, or some other physical characteristic than you are for your ability to perform in the room."

In my experience, this is absolutely true—frustrating, yes, but true! From a purely business standpoint, casting directors want to find the right person for any given job as efficiently as possible, and to do that they need to remember only the right people, and they want nothing more than for you to be that person each time—it would only make their job easier.

What this means is that the casting directors, producers, whomever, are rooting for you each time you walk into that room or onto that stage! Think about that for a second—what an enormous mental and reality leap it is from "Will they think I'm good enough?" to "We both (they and I) really want me to be the answer for their problem!" If you're able to make that transition in your mind, you go from a situation in which one person (you) is self-consciously hoping you're right for the job, to a situation in which everyone in the room is excitedly anticipating that you will be. Imagine the performance you would give at an audition if you knew ahead of time that everyone is on your side!

For me, this realization in 1997 marked a significant transition, and that year alone I was hired for two national commercials, I joined Russia's highest-selling band on tour, and I landed a recurring role on *The Guiding Light*. A few months later, in 1998, I booked my first role in a major motion picture *(Shaft Returns)* and my first lead role in a made-for-TV movie *(2GE+HER)*.

But . . . I'm Not Getting Anywhere

For starters, you're probably already far more successful than you think you are! And there's another perhaps not-so-obvious reason our emotions stand in the way of training our focus where it needs to be, and it goes back to perspective. It's extremely easy to lose sight of our own successes and accomplishments and fall into the trap of, "I'm not getting anywhere," and in my experience, nothing destroys momentum like the false impression that you're not getting anywhere.

I found myself in a mini–life slump not so long ago, one of many I've had throughout my career (as all people do). To break the slump, I did what I always do and that's to sign up for stuff, literally anything and everything that interested me. Those are the only two requirements I ever give myself.

I knew I needed new experiences, new perspectives, new knowledge (any knowledge) and a change of scenery. I also felt like I needed to improve my long-term financial security, so one of the things I signed up for was a real estate investing course.

As part of the training, I had to fill out a weekly questionnaire about the accomplishments of my previous week. To understate it, I was shocked: I felt so mediocre just before filling out the questionnaire, but when I completed it, I realized I really *had* accomplished a lot that week. In actuality, I was over-achieving, even when I felt like a failure.

That exercise cured me, once and for all, of the disease I call "I'm not getting anywhere-itis." I also learned an extremely valuable lesson:

> **It is vitally important to have a way of reflecting on your regular accomplishments and achievements, especially when you're feeling inadequate or stuck.**

This is but one component of the art of self-reflection, but for now let's just say that it's crucial to never let your own momentum wane and your focus become distracted simply because you've forgotten how much you are already accomplishing daily.

Breaking a Success Slump

Bottom line: the quickest way to fix a slump is to change focus, especially if you believe that the slump is bigger than it is, or worse, if you're not actually in a slump but your attitude is tricking you into thinking you are. To cure this, you will need to start reflecting on a regular basis. I know I wish I had earlier!

On the next page is a simple form that will help you do this. Some people journal, some receive feedback from friends, but the most powerful way I've found to establish a useful focus is to write it.

Weekly Questionnaire

Date:_____

What would be the headline for your week as it pertains to your biggest goal? (Example "Evan Farmer Moves to NYC to Break into Entertainment!")

_____

What were your week's goals?

_____

What specific things did you do this week toward your goals?

_____

What were your successes this week?

_____

What were your greatest challenges this week?

_____

What's the most important thing(s) you learned this week?

_____

What are you going to accomplish/do next week?

_____

There's only one rule to make this work for you, and that one rule is to do it . . . anyway. There's that word *anyway* again. It's there to offset the excuses I already know are coming, because I've used them too. And please don't kid yourself by thinking you'll just do it in your head and move on. Take time and write it. Otherwise, it just doesn't work.

Magnification

The second main challenge to establishing and maintaining a useful and effective focus in entertainment is the art of magnification: specifically, knowing when to focus on small details and when to focus on the big picture. The truth is, you really have to know how and when to do both. You can't just "not sweat the small stuff," all the time because after all, "God is in the details." But you also can't spend all of your precious time sorting through the details either, because then you'd never take the big steps required for a career.

When to Focus: Big or Small

Besides being an emotional recalibrator, the weekly exercise on the previous page is also one of your best tools for figuring out if you've become trapped in the swamp of sweating all the small stuff, or if you're throwing random career darts around without enough focus on the big picture: your target.

The second best way to maintain a laser focus on the most effective tasks/issues is to ask a mentor how you're doing; whether that person is a trusted relative, friend, agent, manager, etc. The key is to choose your mentors wisely; remember . . . always consider the source! As I'll discuss in the final chapter, who we choose to surround ourselves with is one of the biggest determiners of success in entertainment (or any field for that matter).

Virtual Mentors

The third way to stay on the focus road-map is to continuously measure your actions and focus against the career paths of the great successes in your field. We don't always have access to great mentors in our personal lives, but that doesn't matter in the least if you know how to surround yourself with virtual mentors.

You can do this by simply asking and finding answers to a question like *What did [any great successful entertainer you admire] do when they were at the stage of their career/life that I am now?*

This will almost always give you a remarkably accurate picture of whether or not you are in alignment. If not, it will tell you what you probably *should* be focusing on instead. Answer this question using a few names of people you admire, and the picture will become crystal clear!

Go on an Information Diet

We live in an information age. This can be an extremely useful thing, and it can be an extremely dangerous trap. It used to be that information was so difficult to come by that we simply went about our lives and hoped that whatever information we had was good enough. Now we have unlimited information at our fingertips, so the problem becomes finding the *good* information—that's a very tough problem. It's way too easy to either get wrapped up in meaningless information or adopt the most convenient information without vetting its usefulness first. The antidote is simple: less information overall.

It may seem somewhat ironic that Steve Jobs, the cofounder of Apple and the undisputed brains behind the company's success, not only agreed with this idea but credited a large part of his own success to managing the overload with a single word: no.

As the closing keynote speaker of Apple's worldwide developer conference back in 1997, Steve Jobs stated a refrain that had become central to his own personal principles for success: "Focusing is about saying no." In 2003, at another speech, Jobs explained further, "People think focus means saying yes to the thing you've got to focus on. But that's not what it means at all. It means saying no to the hundred other good ideas that there are. You have to pick carefully."

Information overload can paralyze you and distract you, and it almost never helps you. The only way to prevent it is going on an "information diet," a concept that has evolved as people have begun to try to take control back from the technology-media onslaught—in other words, learning to say no to anything that doesn't immediately add value to our goals.

In this day and age, we naturally tend to greatly overestimate the quantity of information we really need or that can even be used effectively. We incorrectly worry that someone else knows something we don't and that it will hurt us. Instead we need to concentrate on knowing merely what we *need to know* in order to succeed.

Besides, if we don't consciously think about what to focus on, human nature tends to drive us toward feel-good information: gossip, trivia, news, etc. Even bad news makes us feel better, because we think, Hey at least I'm not in their shoes!

If you want your career to be supercharged, defined by huge leaps, you need to learn to limit the sheer volume of information you receive.

This means: turn off the TV, quit playing that video game, get off the computer, and put down the rag-mags. I'm not advocating being ill-informed about the events of the day, but I am advocating one simple rule: If you need more information to do your civic duty or to attend to your family, yourself, or your career, then seek out only the information you need to do it.

For example, if I just voted at the recent election, I really don't need to watch ten hours of political news a day. Yes, we need distractions in life to unwind and have fun, but today more than ever we need to be in control of it. Left unattended, information overload will turn us into the mediocre, average neighbor we all know . . . and that is not what you are after, is it?

How much is enough? Try going completely dark for a week or two and you will quickly find out what information deserves your attention and what you can honestly live without.

When I started out in entertainment, we didn't have cell phones, but I did just fine. We used to not have email, and yet I managed. Try the information diet and you'll quickly find yourself with so much time that it's almost uncomfortable. Good! Use that spare time toward training, rehearsing, research, networking, building a financial foundation, learning a new skill, getting eight hours of sleep a night, getting into better shape, or just having more fun. This alone will increase your chances of success exponentially!

Warning: you'll probably have to repeat this information diet every so often, just like a regular diet. But that's normal.

Props

One of the best techniques for staying on point and focused in the right direction is the use of props. My favorite story that demonstrates the power of this technique is that of Jim Carrey, the wildly successful comedian and actor, who wrote himself a check for an astronomical amount in 1987, long before he'd had any significant success in Hollywood.

As the story goes, the then twenty-five-year-old struggling comic drove his beat-up car into the Hollywood hills. Sitting on Mulholland Drive, overlooking the city of Los Angeles, Carrey wrote himself a check for ten million dollars. He dated it "Thanksgiving 1995" and added the notation: "for acting services rendered." That check sat in his wallet for another seven years as a reminder to himself of his mission.

By 1994, Carrey had easily earned enough money to cash the check several times over, and as a final gesture to the father he adored, he placed it in his jacket pocket at his funeral. By 1995, his target date, Carrey was earning as much as twenty million dollars per film!

Jim Carrey's story is as open and brazen as the characters he portrays, but one thing I've discovered over the years is that almost every successful entertainer I have ever met, interviewed, or studied has their own "ten-million-dollar check."

Mine was a small rock my mother gave me with a stork painted on it in black ink. According to Native American tradition, the stork is a symbol that represents happiness, prosperity, children, gratitude, and filial duty.

My mother gave it to me the year I moved to New York with a note describing how this same rock, given to her by her friend when she was first diagnosed with breast cancer, helped remind her of her single goal, which was to beat the cancer so that she could spend precious time with her kids. Although her diagnosis in 1990 was terminal, by 1995 she was officially declared in full remission! She had beaten the cancer, and now she was passing the rock on to me at a time when the odds of success in entertainment also seemed overwhelming.

That rock lived in my pocket for five years as a constant reminder of what I was there to accomplish. Literally every time I searched my pocket for change or a subway token or felt the little lump protrude as I sat down, I was remotivated, encouraged, and refocused. Like Jim Carrey did with his father, I had made a silent vow to my mother to never give up on my dream and to stay on point.

Props are like friends that are there when we're the most alone. Because they are so simple and singular, they are the best kind of friend when our minds want to stray off course. They have one message, and it never disappears: "Remember your mission!"

A prop can be anything, a picture posted on your fridge, a token, a book, anything, as long as it symbolizes something powerful to you and is directly linked to your mission, which I imagine is to be the successful artist you dream of being.

There is a second "prop" that you absolutely cannot succeed without, however: the right vocabulary. I'll cover that in the next chapter.

Rule 4: Adopt a winning perspective by developing an active optimism and by learning to direct your focus to your advantage by using the weekly self-reflection exercise, by going on an information diet, and through the use of props.

Sticks and Stones and Wishful Thinking

O NE OF THE most successful and famous con artists of all time is a man named Frank Abagnale, Jr. His story inspired the 2002 film *Catch Me If You Can,* based on the book of the same name. It starred Leonardo DiCaprio as Frank and Tom Hanks as Carl Hanratty, the FBI agent who finally caught him. As the story goes, Frank was able to successfully impersonate an airline pilot, a teaching assistant, a doctor, and an attorney. When I say impersonate, I mean he actually took controls of an airliner for Pan Am, taught sociology at Brigham Young University, acted as a resident supervisor at a hospital in Georgia, and worked at a legitimate law firm in Louisiana.

Why does this matter? Because he did all of this without any training whatsoever. He was not a genius either. He was able to do it by simply learning the vocabulary of each profession and by wielding that vocabulary with such confidence that no reasonable person would ever question him. This should be very exciting news, especially if you're an aspiring actor, because that's acting at its finest! But it's also valuable information because Frank proved something crucial, albeit in a very high-stakes and destructive way:

To be a thing is to speak like a thing.

This lesson is simple: become an expert on the language of the industry you're pursuing, starting today! I've got a twist on an old familiar saying that I believe captures this reality:

Sticks and stones may break your bones, but words can make *or* break you.

So how do you master this vocabulary? The same way Frank Abagnale did: listen very carefully to the words used by those in the business you are pursuing; ask a lot of questions (after all, you're not a con man—no need for secrecy), and read as much about your industry as possible.

Obviously knowing and being able to correctly and confidently use the right words or vocabulary is important, as Frank's story indicates, but the wrong words, especially the words we use when speaking to ourselves, can break you. I have found that the most successful artists have learned to eliminate these "destructive" words from their vocabulary entirely.

The Power of Words: Words Affect Belief

Don't believe it when they tell you that "words can never hurt you." Words can literally destroy lives, cause wars, and change history. Behind every stick and stone is a taunt or a threat, and you don't have to look far to find stories of how verbal abuse has decimated someone's psyche, self confidence, will to live, or even willingness to commit murder!

It's easy to see and sympathize when someone verbally abuses another person, but what we all too frequently take for granted are the ways in which we constantly verbally abuse ourselves without even opening up our mouths!

Take an audition where you didn't get the job, for example.

Some typical words you might say to yourself in your head might include: *I'm terrible under pressure! I'm not good enough! They were jerks! That was a waste of time.* You know the drill. What usually happens next is exactly the opposite, and, as a result, a negative version of the autosuggestion exercise outlined earlier: you end up subconsciously seeking proof that these statements you made to yourself (generated by your emotions) are true. This becomes a negative self-fulfilling prophecy, and that will always take you further away from what it was you wanted in the first place: getting the job!

Researchers in the field of human behavior have many theories as to why this is so, but the one thing they all agree on is that negative words, especially the ones we use to talk to ourselves, simply do not serve us when it comes to achieving anything.

By the same token, words can create infinite possibilities. I'll never forget the day Chris, a classmate in elementary school, turned to me and said, "You should audition for the lead [role in a musical] 'cause you can sing." Without those words, I may never have considered musical theatre or, more specifically, singing to be a possible career choice. No one had ever told me, "You can sing," and, until then, I had never believed it.

What successful people know is that words become things. High achievers literally use words to create their results. This is a far different mindset from the way the average person uses words, which is to simply convey a reaction to things. This reaction is not only disempowering but is also often damaging to your goal.

For example, someone who knows how to use words to create his or her desired results might say the following after the same audition instead: *What did I learn from this? In a numbers game (which auditioning ultimately is), this was just one more number closer to getting an offer! I'm getting so much better at handling rejection!*

Whereas the first response certainly got you no closer to

your goal, what this new response created with a simple change of language are the following positive results:

1.   Useful information *(What did I learn?)*
2.   A step closer to getting the next job *(Confidence)*
3.   The critical skill of handling rejection *(Asset)*

This approach creates these results with words rather than focusing on only one possible result: getting that specific job.

Break the Pattern

So how do you break the negative pattern? Try this: the next time you hear yourself saying the kinds of negative things in the example above, stop and ask yourself: Is this really true? What else would I have to believe for this to really be true? You'll quickly find that, more often than not, you're way off base in your assessment anyway.

After all, if you were, in fact, really terrible, you probably wouldn't have gotten the audition in the first place (unless of course you're being used for laughs on a reality show). If the folks conducting the audition (the casting director, for example) really *were* jerks, then you would also have to believe that their entire world revolved around hurting people. If it were, in fact, a waste of time, then you would have to believe that you are utterly incapable of learning anything new as well as totally incapable of valuing your own time.

In addition to all of this, remember that we always learn more from disappointments than from our big wins. With a victory, all we ever have to do to get the same result is to repeat the same actions, so no new learning is necessary! Disappointments, on the other hand, teach us what we need to fix or do differently to win next time.

To begin this process of vocabulary rehab, there are two words you need to stop using right away: *hope* and *failure.*

Hope: You Can't Lose It if You Never Had It in the First Place

The first critical distinction that needs to be made as you begin your journey toward retraining your mind is the huge divide between *hope* and *certainty*.

Think back to chapter 4 when I had you ask yourself the question *Do you believe you will succeed?*

What was your first and immediate reaction? More than likely, there was some level of hesitation (if you're a normal human being). But we're not after being normal. Normal people have boring lives, and normal people don't become stars. Stars have all learned to take their thinking up a notch, and that includes a new and improved vocabulary.

> **In your heart right now, you may not be 100 percent certain of your imminent success, and that's OK. You cannot, however, afford to just hope for it anymore either.**

To become a believer, you often have to fake it first; to act *as if* it were impossible to fail, as Charles F. Kettering (inventor of the electric starter) advises. I'll cover this skill (and one of the great secrets of the über-successful) in great detail in chapter 8, but the important thing to learn here is that it always begins with words.

When you fully believe, you are not hoping. Believers are certain of a positive outcome, and they're the ones who eventually get that outcome. Note the difference between the following statements: "I *will* star in a major motion picture," and "I *hope to* star in a major motion picture." The difference is this: when you hope for something, you're allowing for the possibility for it to *not* happen. This will not serve you in any productive way.

Here's an example. Let's say a friend of yours hopes to star in a major motion picture and gives herself a fifty-fifty chance of it happening and three years to do it (a random deadline I still hear people give themselves to this day).

On the other hand, say you have another friend in the same boat who is certain he will star in a major motion picture and gives himself a 100 percent chance of success. If these were two of your friends, which one would you bet on?

I know who I'd bet on! You may remember me telling you in the introduction about how, when I got to New York in 1995, I found myself surrounded by far more talented people who were "out to give it a shot." By contrast, I was there to do it . . . period. I never *tried* to succeed in entertainment. I didn't *hope* to make it. I *decided* to be a successful entertainer. I used certainty to my advantage. And so did Zach Braff, Ed Norton, and Kristin Chenoweth, who were also just starting out in New York City at that same time.

Not convinced yet? OK, let's assume for the sake of argument that a sophisticated computer could determine that, unbeknownst to them, your two friends in the example above really did have exactly a fifty-fifty chance of realizing the same goal.

The hoper will no doubt stop at the first sign that she feels her 50 percent chance is up—perhaps at that arbitrary three-year mark. Meanwhile the certain friend, at that same three-year junction, would simply believe that his goal hasn't come to fruition yet and would keep going. The frustrated hoper quits while the certain friend goes to one more audition and voilà—goal achieved!

This is exactly what happened to me in 1998. Although I was certain—from age six—that I was going to be a successful entertainer one day, after three years of getting beat up by rejection and close calls that never seemed to go my way, I was definitely starting to feel defeated. I had even expressed as much to my agent, who encouraged me to go on one more audition before I left town for a much-needed break—it was so last minute that I actually went to the audition on the way to the airport! The result? I got as far as Dallas, where I was changing planes; there, I got the call that I had been offered the role of Christian Bale's friend in the upcoming movie *Shaft Returns*. That "one last" audition changed everything and was the beginning of a series of breaks for me.

Recently I saw Robert Pattinson, the star of the blockbuster *Twilight* film series, being interviewed by Matt Lauer on the *Today Show.* I was blown away when Pattinson revealed that he had decided to quit acting the day before the *Twilight* audition but went to this last one anyway.

I heard the exact same thing in an interview with James Van Der Beek, who starred on *Dawson's Creek,* one of the most successful drama series of the 1990s. They're both now multimillionaires, with the ability to work or not work in their chosen craft indefinitely as they choose. All because both said, "OK, just *one more* try. . . ."

The truth is, it would be impossible to know for sure if I was truly close to being done with the business when I hopped the flight out of New York, or if Robert Pattinson or James Van Der Beek were either. That's just how we felt when we showed up that one more time—but I for one am sure glad I did!

The Audacity of Certainty

In light of the above, I propose you would do well to lose the word *hope* from your vocabulary. In life, the only people who never achieve their goals are those who stop trying. And when you stop trying, you inadvertently also lose all of the other possibilities that would have been created in the continued pursuit of your goal, whether relevant to your main goal or not.

In fact, many times along the way I found myself presented with another opportunity I never expected and chose to put my original goal on hold for a bit. This is one reason I've been blessed to work in so many different entertainment genres; an opportunity just came up and it looked fun, so I took it! Sometimes I returned to achieve the original goal later (often with the help and momentum of the experience I had just gained from the unexpected opportunity) and sometimes I realized that the previous goal wasn't an important one for me anymore. In either case, I didn't fall short of the goal as a hoper fears might happen, because I was still the one determining a very desirable outcome.

This leads me to my next critical point . . .

You Will Never Fail Again!

Earlier, I shared the second truth of the entertainment business: "There is no such thing as failure—only information that we can use to our benefit." Starting today, do yourself a huge favor and completely eliminate the word *failure* from your vocabulary.

Here's a better substitution to use anytime you try something that doesn't provide you with your immediately desired results: useful information.

We can use information, but we can't use failure. Failure is an ending. Information is a new beginning. This goes for all incarnations for the word *failure* as well, including rejection, denial, dismissal, elimination, botched, catastrophe, disappointment, etc.

> I have not failed. I've just found ten thousand ways that won't work.
> —*Thomas Edison*

Information steers us in a more refined direction and lets us know what we need more of and less of. It clues us into what to pay attention to, what not to pay attention to anymore, what works, and what doesn't. In fact information is our best mentor—available 24 hours a day, 365 days a year, and it is exclusively ours if we want it to be. This gives us a distinct advantage.

In Edison's estimation, he was merely "informed" of ten thousand ways the light bulb didn't work. Furthermore this information was his very own trade secret. Anyone else with the same goal was doomed to repeat the same steps, which for Edison was a huge advantage toward being the *first* to make it work! Risk takers learn, learners succeed, and those who succeed get all of the rewards.

Harrison Ford may not have gone to ten thousand auditions before he was cast in *Star Wars* (though I'm sure the number is close) but he was out there going at it for ten years before it happened!

As simplistic as this concept is, and as common sense as this all sounds, it's amazing how immune we are to the message because we are constantly bombarded with the pervasive lie that failure even exists. The only way to fight the lie is to avoid it as much as possible (especially in the media) and to consistently remind ourselves of the fact that every undesired result is only information—information that will give us a great advantage on the way to success. Once we have truly internalized this fact, much of our fear of failure, rejection, disappointment, etc., will simply disappear.

One of the biggest ways to apply this new approach—effective immediately—is in your auditions. My agent Mark, one of my greatest supporters, offered me this advice:

Don't audition for the job you're going to, but for the one down the road.

From my experience, I've learned to view every audition as simply practice. Priority number one for me is never to simply "get the job" I'm auditioning for, though that's often one of the outcomes. Instead, my only goal today is to give a great audition and leave a positive and professional lasting impression that might help me get a job down the road. This not only takes much of the pressure off my immediate performance, but it ensures that I stayed focused on the only thing I can control, and that is doing my best at any given moment.

This seemingly small change in my approach has made me a lot of money and has allowed me to win jobs in several cases when there were far more talented and far better trained candidates in the running. I was just best in that moment, because I had less to lose!

Ask any working person in the arts and they'll tell you they always get offered more work

> The Chinese use two brush strokes to write the word *crisis*. One brush stroke stands for the word *danger*; the other for *opportunity*.
>
> —*John F. Kennedy*

when they either don't need the job, couldn't take the job due to other commitments, or don't even want the job. This is not Murphy's Law at work, it's because your brain automatically goes to that unpressurized, relaxed, and optimized state of mind when you truly don't need the outcome to be "getting that one job." The great news is that, with practice, it's possible to remain in that state of mind all the time!

The Magic List

This process of learning a new language and un-learning a negative and counterproductive one requires a lot of dedication. While you are out discovering the vocabulary of the trade, which is a fairly simple process, the most difficult thing to do is to retrain your brain to automatically substitute and eventually eliminate the counterproductive words.

Just about the only way to do this is to make yourself totally aware of this negative habit (which so many of us have), and the best technique I know of for doing that is to carry around a pad for a few weeks and make a list of the words you hear coming out of your mouth (as well as the ones that never make it that far—no cheating!) that you now know to be counterproductive and negative. Then, all you need to do is find a useful and positive word or phrase to replace it with.

Below are a few examples from an old list of mine to help get you in the zone:

- *failure* became *information* or *one step closer*
- *hope* became *certain* or *determined*
- *can't* became *will* or *doing it*
- *rejected* became *informed* or *determined*
- *hate* became *prefer* or *not interested*
- *depressed* became *feeling better* or *getting over it*
- *angry* became *fixing it* or *I'm gonna show them!*
- *terrible* became *unexpected* or *not for me*

- *insulted* became *misunderstood* or *misinformed*
- *waste* became *irrelevant* or *information*

Once you actually start swapping out these words, you may notice something else happening as well: you'll start to notice other people around you abusing the negatives. This is critically important for two reasons. The first is that this will kick your own transformation into high gear because, frankly, it will probably start to bother you a lot. Secondly, it will cast some light on the people you're surrounded by.

This second part is so vitally important to breaking in and staying in that I will devote a whole chapter to it later on. For now, just think of how difficult it is to change when everyone around you isn't doing the same.

If you want to quit smoking, any expert will tell you to do it along with your friends or *get new friends*! Your chances of success are statistically almost zero otherwise. This simply means that you either need to get those around you to improve their vocabulary and thinking with you, or you need to stop spending time with them. Period. There are plenty of people out there who use a vocabulary that will bring you down all day, but there are also plenty of others who will further inspire you to improve yours exponentially. They're usually easy to find—they are the people who are going somewhere fast.

Why I Love Quotes: A Final Word About Words

You've probably noticed my abundant use of quotes throughout this book already. Quotes have been my own personal coach throughout my life for dealing with any difficult scenario, both related to entertainment and otherwise.

Put simply, quotes are *power words* constructed into *power phrases*. They're easy-to-remember reminders of the empowering phrases uttered by people who are far more successful, intelligent, and far more experienced than me. Best of all, they can save you the time of not remaking mistakes already made by others because they are catchy and easy to remember.

So the next time you want to swap out a negative thought for a positive one, do a computer search of a few key words from your notepad exercise relating to your situation, like *disappointment* or *rejection,* and add the word *quote* and you'll likely find some great and wise anecdotes.

Once we eliminate the negative words and phrases from our vocabulary, a curious thing starts happening; we begin to see things differently. Possibilities and opportunities suddenly come to us; we become more imaginative, creative, successful; and, as a by-product of that success, we become happier.

Being a much happier person also has a powerful tangential effect. People like being around happy people, and since people hire people they want to be around, they hire happy ones. Wouldn't you?

> **Rule 5: Become an expert on the language of the industry you're pursuing starting today! Lose the words *hope* and *failure* from your vocabulary and replace all nonproductive words with empowering ones. Start surrounding yourself with people who use vocabulary to their advantage as well.**

Ten Questions All Successful Artists Ask

T HE PROCESS OF thinking is nothing more than asking ourselves questions. We literally walk around all day and night having conversations with ourselves that begin with a question:

- What did he/she mean?
- Am I in the mood for Chinese food or pizza?
- Do I really have to get out of bed now?
- What will I say when I get there?

These internal questions usually require another question and another and another until we have an answer. Then we often question *that* answer, and so on and so forth, until we're satisfied. It's how we're wired!

Because of this, questions, as I mentioned earlier, also direct our focus. As in the example I gave earlier in describing how I acquired an agent, I wasn't satisfied with the answer you typically get to the question *How do I get an agent?* (Find work first and then invite an agent to watch you perform.) So I asked another question instead: *What's a better, and faster, way to get an agent?* This led me to focus on the agent's needs, and the next logical question: *How do I fulfill those perceived needs best?* My focus remained laser-sharp and was dictated by the quality questions I started asking from the start, which leads me to my next point:

The quality of the questions you ask determines the quality of answers you get.

Want to know how to become a world-famous and celebrated entertainer, for example? Well . . . that's a good question to start with! Your next question should probably be something like: *How did [insert your idol here] do it?* And so on.

Be careful, though. If you ask lousy questions, you'll get lousy answers. For example, if I had found out that someone waiting tables with me just signed on with a top-tier music agent and I spent my time asking questions like *Why is she always so lucky? Why am I so lame? Why do I even bother trying?* Then I'll end up with lousy answers—even if they're not true. *She's just lucky. I'm lame because I'm no good. This is a waste of my time.* Our brain will merely accommodate us as it always does, and the next thing we know we're in a self-defeating downward spiral.

The Difference

At the heart of all bad questions are assumptions. So to prevent bad questions, the first thing you need to do is to eliminate assumptions and only deal in facts. After all, if you asked a few good questions, you'd likely find out that the girl you wait tables with is probably not that lucky after all! In fact, she may even be a great resource for information you could use to get a music agent yourself. You'd also realize that you're not lame, you just haven't done what she's done yet!

With this in mind, I'm going to jump right into the *Ten Questions All Successful Artists Ask.* As you read them, keep in mind this one final truth: Questions are also only useful if you take physical action along with them. I know a lot of extremely talented artists who spend a lot of time asking a million great questions and get fantastic answers, but who never act on them. That's tragic.

1. What do I really want?

This is the true starting place of your career. This is also where most people who never succeed mess up first. Why? They never have anything more than a vague notion of what they really want specifically. Instead, if you ask most people what they want, they'll say things like, "I just want to be happy," or "I want to be rich and famous," or "I want to be an actor, singer, comedian, director, etc."

> Happiness is not a goal; it is a by-product.
> —*Eleanor Roosevelt*

But trust me when I tell you that these vague answers are never going to help you. For this question to hold any useful power, your answers must be extremely specific and true to yourself.

After all it's entirely possible to be an actor, singer, comedian, and director and yet not have a career. You may not need to be a successful entertainer in order to be happy, but it certainly can be a great by-product!

I have a lot of friends who are great actors, singers, comics, and directors, but you've never heard of them and they can't support themselves on their craft alone. So what do you really want—specifically? Jim Carrey made it 100 percent clear to himself exactly what he wanted and in what time frame when he wrote his famous check to himself for $10 million, dated it "Thanksgiving 1995," and put "for acting services rendered" in the memo space.

The two critical elements your answer requires in order to be useful are an *extremely specific description* ($10 million for acting services rendered) and an *exact time frame* (Thanksgiving 1995). Do this with each and every one of your goals!

You will also need to get in the habit of rechecking your answers over time; your opportunities and your life in general will often change independently of your goals. Mine, for example, changed tremendously after I had my first child.

As I've mentioned before, I'll often get an opportunity I can't refuse on the way to my original goal that will change everything. This simply means that even though your answers are specific and time-based, you need to remain fluid and keep asking yourself question one: *What do I want?*

Purpose

2. Why do I want it?

This is the second-most-important question that every single successful artist you have ever heard of asks, simply because without a strong enough reason you will never make it past the first rejection.

It's not enough to *kind of want* your dream, or even to *really* want it! If succeeding in your field of entertainment isn't an all-encompassing obsession, born out of the greatest desire to show the world who you are and what you're capable of (or something equivalent to that) well . . . find a career that does stir that up inside of you.

> In order to succeed, your desire for success should be greater than your fear of failure.
>
> —*Bill Cosby*

This career requires a little more drive than most as a direct result of the sheer amount of rejection you'll be forced to overcome and endure on a constant basis. But here's a little good news reminder: most people are so frightened of this one aspect that they never really try, even if they pretend to. This means that there is far less competition out there than you may think.

Don't have a strong enough reason yet? No problem—go get one! Asking yourself a few other questions like the following examples may help you find one.

- Want to prove someone wrong about you? Success is the sweetest revenge!

- Do you really want to remain poor, middle class, average etc.? Simply wanting more out of life than was expected of them has motivated many successful entertainers!

- Do you want to be remembered when you die? Leaving a lasting legacy can be tremendously powerful to many artists.

- Do you want to inspire millions of people you've never even met? This has always been one of my deepest desires.

There are an infinite number of questions you can ask yourself to get you to that all-encompassing "why," but you cannot get around the process of exploring and ultimately answering this for yourself. Prepare for the possibility that this soul-searching process may take a lot of effort and a bit of time to sort out, but do it . . . anyway!

3. Is what I'm doing/want in line with my values?

One of the most profound concepts I have ever encountered, which speaks to every choice we make in our careers and lives, comes from Stephen Covey's groundbreaking 1989 book, *The 7 Habits of Highly Effective People.*

Stephen's Habit #2: Begin with the End in Mind, suggests that the reader picture his/her own funeral many years from now and imagine what each of the important people in your life would say about you as they stood over your casket. More importantly, he suggests that you concentrate on what you would like them to say. The results of this exercise are a snapshot of your deepest values and should guide every decision, particularly the difficult ones you come across, for the rest of your life. Wow!

In fact, this is the exact exercise I do *every time* I have a difficult decision to make, and it usually makes my answer crystal clear. Do I cancel my charity commitment for the great work opportunity, or do I want to be remembered as a man of my word? It's in these answers that legacies are born.

This also involves appreciating the value of time as well. There are a million resources on time management out there—enough to make you dizzy—but one thing is hard to argue with, and that's the fact that we need to constantly remind ourselves how precious little of it we have. If we're constantly aware of this reality, I believe that we, as instinctual beings, naturally make the better choices each day that take us toward our goals. Below is a powerful poem that I think sums this idea up quite well.

The Value of Time

Author Unknown

To realize the value of ten years, ask a newly divorced couple.

To realize the value of four years, ask a graduate.

To realize the value of one year, ask a student who has failed an exam.

To realize the value of nine months, ask a mother who gave birth to a stillborn.

To realize the value of one month, ask a mother who gave birth to a premature baby.

To realize the value of one week, ask an editor of a weekly news-paper.

To realize the value of one hour, ask the lovers who are waiting to meet.

To realize the value of one minute, ask a person who has missed the train, bus, or plane.

To realize the value of one second, ask a person who has survived an accident.

To realize the value of one millisecond, ask the person who has won a silver medal in the Olympics.

Time waits for no one. Treasure every moment you have.

4. How did [successful person] do it?

I'm always shocked at how many people don't ask this question constantly and obsessively. Instead, they seem to want someone close to them such as their drama teacher; their guitar teacher; or their opinionated uncle, parent, or friend to guide them toward their dreams. The only problem is that if you're like me, none of your close connections have achieved anything in *the business* of entertainment!

The best way to learn how to do something is to ask someone who is the best at doing it. Then ask another, and another, and another, until *you* are the expert.

Obvious patterns will emerge that will always seem to magically answer the two questions I get asked the most by aspiring artists I meet: What do I need to do first to become a(n)_____? What do I need to do next?

When I started out in 1995, the Internet wasn't a factor and there certainly were no smartphones (we were still using pagers), but I had my two favorite resources: the bookstore and a subscription to *Biography* magazine, in which I read everything I could about the careers of the greatest entertainers of all time. That's how I learned 90 percent of everything I needed to know to break into every genre I've ever worked in (and I've worked in most). Today, you can do this research just about anywhere there's an Internet connection!

5. How can I do it better, faster, and more efficiently?

If you're like me, it's not enough to simply learn what Harrison Ford did and then repeat those steps if you want to be an actor. In fact, Ford himself could probably tell you a few things from experience that he could have done better, faster, more efficiently, or even not done along the way. Those are the real nuggets you're looking for.

There will be times when you simply need to use your creativity to figure this out, as I did when seeking an agent. From the great entertainers I researched, I knew I needed an agent, but I devised my own creative route to getting one fast.

6. What are my assets?

This is all about taking stock in yourself and capitalizing on your strengths. It's also about thinking like a chess player to some degree. A few years after I first got to New York, I was auditioning for and getting many callbacks for Broadway shows for roles that always seemed to go to soap stars, pop stars, and other big names. While frustrating, this was a good thing as well, for two reasons. First, I realized that getting close was good enough for my agent to continue to pay attention to me (asset). Also, it encouraged me to become one of the "big names" who always get the job regardless of how well the audition went (goal adjustment: an information asset).

I quickly realized another asset of mine was versatility, so I made sure to audition for anything and everything my agents mentioned, and I quickly developed a reputation as a guy who could and would do anything and everything. This led to me touring Russia with Ha-Ha, screen testing to host *America's Funniest Home Videos* with Daisy Fuentes, a Ford truck commercial in which I faked playing bass guitar, film and TV roles, and eventually, after building enough name recognition, I was finally offered a lead role in the Broadway production of *Cinderella,* costarring Jamie-Lynn Sigler (well known at that time for her role on the hit HBO show *The Sopranos*).

In the end, I turned the show down due to contractual conflicts, but it sure felt good to have finally cracked the code I was trying to break. This all came down to constantly evaluating my assets and setting aside my weaknesses and disadvantages.

7. Is this [commonly held or your own] assumption true?

I've already mentioned the need to eliminate assumptions to avoid bad questions. Throughout your career, you will encounter an endless stream of advice and assumptions, some of it solicited, most of it not. My advice on this is to question *everything,* listen to your instincts, and do research in order to vet it out. Completely disregard anything that doesn't pass immediate muster.

One of the great traps of this industry are incorrect but widely held assumptions, because so much misinformation surrounds the industry by design. It's one of the few industries that can sell advertising in magazines and during TV programs that consist entirely of people just talking *about* the industry, even though most of that information is false, misleading, or useless. By simply being aware of this and by asking the above question, you will join an elite group that knows the truth.

8. What's the worst that could happen?

I can't tell you how many times this question metaphorically talked me off the ledge. This industry requires taking some fairly uncomfortable risks. This question alone can help you work through the anxiety of taking many of these necessary risks by focusing on reason and logic.

Once you realize that *this* audition, *this* meeting, *this* move to LA won't end your life or your future, it's far easier to take that next step. Most of the time you'll realize that this "huge" thing actually has very little long-term negative bearing, even if it all blows up horribly in your face!

9. How can I use this result and/or turn this around? What did I learn?

This question is vital to a successful frame of mind and to moving forward in any situation in which we didn't get the most ideal result we were looking for. It's the question that keeps us moving in the right direction toward our ultimate goal, and it will be the question you need to ask yourself the most often.

10. How am I doing overall? Is what I'm doing working?

This is the broader question that relates to the question above. While it's critical to dissect most unintended results, it's just as critical to step back from time to time and ask this broader question.

I don't recommend always doing this alone either, as we're most often so intimately embedded in our own lives emotionally that it's extremely difficult to see the forest for the trees. This is one question I highly recommend asking someone you trust and then really listening intently to discover how far you've come, how on track you really are, and whether you are even still on course anymore at all!

Keep Moving Forward

Using these questions daily to continuously guide you will provide the precise information you need to move forward and eliminate most of the fluff all around us that passes for information. These questions guide us by providing focus and perspective, and they keep us aligned with our vision and our high standards—which will edge you into the 1 percent of all artists who reap 99 percent of the rewards. The next section of this book will focus on acquiring and refining the traits that the most successful artists possess.

Rule 6: Cultivate the habit of regularly asking the ten questions all successful artists ask.

PART III

ADMIT ONE

TRAITS

The First Six-Pack
Belief • Vision • Standards • Optimism • Focus • Purpose

Part II was devoted entirely to the state of mind that is required for success in this industry, specifically the six key foundations of successful thinking, which include:

- The ability to believe in your future success
- The specific vision you have for it coming to fruition
- Having much higher standards for yourself than anyone else has for you
- Your overall optimism in any given scenario that you are in control of your destiny
- Your ability to stay focused on the appropriate task
- Being crystal clear on why you are seeking your vision or goal; in other words—your purpose

The Second Six-Pack
Creative • Self-Motivated • Confident • Decisive
Insatiable • Self-Reflective

Part III will spell out the specific character traits of successful artists that allow them to achieve success beyond most expectations, and to do so with great consistency. What makes these qualities different from the first six-pack is that they each involve a component of physical action and behavior. Adopt them, and you'll be acting and behaving like the great artists who broke in before you.

Acquiring the Six Key Traits of Successful Artists

DO AN INTERNET search for the phrase "successful character traits," and you'll discover endless lists of qualities from a million sources all attempting to capture the magic ingredients for success. Of all of these qualities, a few in particular seem to recur the most, and of these, several seem to be the most commonly held characteristic traits of successful artists. I covered six of them in Part II, as they relate specifically to a way of thinking that can be systematically adopted through practices I have described.

The six traits I'll cover in the next few chapters, however, are just as critical but somehow seem more elusive. These are often qualities that we generally tend to attribute to the personality we're born with. Again they are:

Creative • Self-Motivated • Confident • Decisive • Insatiable • Self-Reflective

We often hear people say things like, "Even as a baby, he/she was just so creative, a self-starter, confident, decisive (often called stubborn), insatiable, self-correcting, etc." The truth is that *all* kids naturally possess these qualities to some degree.

Kids are some of the most creative problem solvers around—just ask a parent whose kid manipulates them before he or she can even talk. Never in the history of man did a baby *not* have an incredible self-motivation to walk. Likewise, kids are fearless; they know what they want, they never seem to get enough, and they're like super-computers when it comes to quickly analyzing something that doesn't work and trying something else.

For many reasons, many adults both young and old lose these traits along the way. Still, if you want to be a successful artist you need to rediscover or cultivate them, and quickly.

The good news is that these traits can be systematically found and/or cultivated. The even better news is that as an artist, you are already likely tapping the right brain with ease, and this is where this process begins.

Creativity

We often think about creativity as it relates to art. It is my assumption that, as an artist, you are already intimately acquainted with your imagination. That's great for the 10 percent side of the 90/10 rule, or the *show* side of show business.

The distinction between the successful working artist and the merely imaginative artist, however, is the ability to use this creative quality to create

> Creativity can solve almost any problem. The creative act, the defeat of habit by originality, overcomes everything.
> —*George Lois, American art director*

possibilities in the 90 percent or *business* side of the equation. This begins simply by looking at every single problem or challenge the same way you approach your art, and then taking action to solve each problem with this insight.

Give Yourself a Big Advantage

You already know how I applied creativity to finding an agent in 1995, but here's another example, from fifteen years later, of how I used creativity to solve the challenge of acquiring the job of hosting and coproducing *CMT's Top 20 Countdown.*

When I moved to Nashville to start setting down roots for my growing family, I looked around and saw very few options for work in television that didn't require me to travel year-round (as I had done with the home makeover shows I'd hosted for the previous seven years). I did, however, notice a local job that I began to covet on the Country Music Television (CMT) network, one of my favorite channels, but alas, it wasn't available as it was occupied by the same host who had held it for eight years.

A few months later, I happened to meet the vice president of new programming for CMT in the elevator of my building, and I knew I had to get a meeting there so that they would at least know who I was should this spot ever open up.

Remembering Dale Carnegie's Principle #5, Talk in terms of the other person's interests, I mentioned that I was also a producer now (our conversation began from her recognizing me as the host of *While You Were Out*) and said that I would love to pitch her my shows. Over the last year or so, I had created some pitch materials for a few adventure reality series. Even though they were designed for networks quite different from CMT, that didn't matter to me. She took the meeting.

To my surprise, almost a year later, the job I coveted became available and—you guessed it—I was called in and asked if I would like to meet with the vice president of the network to discuss it. From this point on is where using my imagination really paid off.

Whenever an opportunity arises, the first thing I do (and the first thing I did here) is to put myself in *their shoes.* I figured if I were the person interviewing me, I'd want to get a feel for me in a meeting; I'd want to see if I looked the part, had a background for the job, possessed a solid knowledge of country music, and was personable. In other words, was I someone I would like to work with? With the confidence of a respectable track record behind me and as a long-time fan of country music, I already felt good about these things.

I'd also want to test me and put me on the spot, since I knew this job would require being able to think on my feet in certain situations, such as interviewing celebrities at awards shows. I thought, if I were him, I'd probably surprise me with a screen test at that meeting, which is exactly what happened. But, as you'll see, I was ready . . . more ready than most.

I immediately took stock in my assets and realized that one skill I was not yet very adept at was reading a teleprompter. I knew I needed to practice if I wanted to nail this potential screen test. So I downloaded some free teleprompter software (a trial offer) on my computer that turns your screen into a scrolling prompter just like the ones used in TV news.

I also wanted to have a distinct advantage with the material I'd be required to read at a screen test. I didn't want to have to cold-read an unfamiliar script like I imagined all of my competition would have to do. I also figured that, *if I were them,* I'd be efficient and simply use the script that was most recently used for the show they had just finished taping that week. So I recorded the show on my DVR from the week prior to my scheduled meeting and transcribed, word for word, what the previous host said. Then I substituted my name into the prompter software and began to practice.

Lastly, I surmised that if I were them, I'd want to hire someone who could not only read a prompter well and present the given material with ease, but also someone who could add their own unique flavor, especially if they were funny. So while rehearsing with this particular script, I came up with and memorized specific jokes and other relevant artist trivia, which I planned to play off as being conjured "in the moment." (If any of this sounds deceptive, consider that this is the exact same routine I go through *now* to prepare *every week* as the consulting producer of the show.)

Now, in playing all of this out the way I did in my imagination, not only was I creatively problem-solving a situation I had yet to encounter, but I was also using the visualization skill that so many professional athletes have used that got them into the Hall of Fame.

Did I know for sure that it would happen this way? No, but that was of little importance, because this process of imagining possible scenarios and then problem-solving them was, in itself, what gave me the extra confidence to take on a totally foreign situation! I was role-playing with myself.

You cannot imagine the feeling of power, control, and confidence that came over me when, sitting in the vice president's office for our meeting, he called in the head of talent and said, "Is the studio ready? Let's throw him in and see how he does."

That moment actually paled in comparison to the moment when they pulled up the script on the prompter and I realized that it was exactly the one I had rehearsed for nearly a full week and had prepped my "impromptu" and "unscripted" jokes and trivia for! And of course I had thoroughly tested out all those jokes on my family with different deliveries first to make sure they were solid.

Later, I found out that they had screen tested at least five hundred people from LA, New York, and Nashville—some very big names too—but in the end I got the job. I also found out later that a key factor in getting the job was my ability to come up with jokes on the spot and under such pressure. What they didn't know at the time was that of course I was under way less pressure than any of the other 499 candidates because, unlike them, I had had the script for a whole week and had planned out, visualized, and rehearsed every second of my "surprise" screen test. I definitely had the overwhelming advantage to say the least—*an advantage that I gave myself.*

In the end, I'm 99 percent sure that I ultimately went much, much, much further than most other candidates to get this job (there are those standards again), and where I placed the majority of those efforts was in the creativity I tapped into in order to control my outcome.

Self-Motivated

This trait always seems to come more easily to some people than others. It likely has more to do with your childhood than anything else. Were you handed everything growing up, or did you have to work hard and fight for what you got? Were your role models handed much of what they had, or did they fight for what they had? The latter group knows the power and sensation of self-reliance.

The bottom line is that once you experience the intoxicating drug of achievement, especially the achievement of providing for yourself, you will always have motivation to seek out more. This starts with becoming more self-reliant than you may already be right now.

I equate this process to skydiving. If you have ever had the experience, as I have, of jumping out of an airplane with nothing more than a parachute, you will also know how human nature rises to the occasion and helps you find that rip cord darn quick.

The same goes for self-reliance in life. Jump out of your comfort nest and you'll find yourself flying. After a while, if it's not already an obvious character trait in you, you'll become addicted to this feeling and want more. That's the essence of being self-motivated, and it starts with a leap.

As I stated in chapter 3, if you're not able to take this very first leap, then frankly this isn't the career for you. It doesn't need to be a skydive the first time out, but a little step is required. This could be anything from supporting yourself financially for the first time, getting your first apartment, or simply taking the reigns of your future career by doing research, taking classes, auditioning for that school play, etc. When you do this, you'll find that each little taste of success will generate a larger desire for more.

Beyond taking that first step into total self-reliance, you can also find powerful motivation elsewhere. For example, every single time I was told I couldn't or was incapable of doing something, I became angry and highly motivated to prove them wrong. In fact, this is perhaps one of the most common themes I hear from success stories!

This also couldn't have been more evident than in the following experience I endured in 1997: after an audition I had for a major network TV pilot that I thought had gone particularly well, I very excitedly headed straight to my agent's building and had him call the network for feedback while I was in his office. Based on my exuberance, both of us were so confident in the great feedback we'd hear that my agent allowed me to listen in silently on an extension.

Big mistake. The verbal lashing that I indirectly endured, and the one my agent took for sending me on the audition in the first place, was among the most painful humiliations I've ever experienced. "He's the worst actor I have ever seen; I promise you he'll never work a single day in television," and "If you ever suggest that I see him again, I'll never see *any* of your other clients ever again." These were just a few of the insults lodged my way. Even thinking about it now, over a decade later, the pain is palpable.

But believe it or not, I'm eternally grateful for that awful experience, as I can't remember ever in my life having such an all-consuming need to prove someone wrong. Every morning, I woke up, channeled that anger, and used it to push me right on through the frustrations, setbacks, and self-doubt. I was Rocky in training.

Two years later, when my success in the MTV movie *2GE+HER* put me in sudden demand, who called my agent to offer me, *without even requiring an audition,* the lead role in a new pilot? You guessed it, the very same casting executive who had told my agent (and unbeknownst to him, me as well) that I would "never work a single day in television."

I had the extreme pleasure of passing on that offer, and as a bonus I was able to use it to increase the salary that MTV was, at the same time, offering me for a twenty-episode series based on the movie. To say the least, my metaphorical middle finger practically ached it was outstretched so high!

Hillary's Finger

A little over a year before winning her first Academy Award in 1999 for her role in *Boys Don't Cry,* actress Hillary Swank was fired from the hit series *Beverly Hills, 90210* because the producers felt she wasn't a good enough actress for the show. I haven't personally had the pleasure of asking her yet, but I'm guessing this had a similar effect on her future career—a career that includes being only one of a small handful of actresses to have been nominated twice for an Academy Award and to win both times, joining Vivien Leigh, Helen Hayes, Sally Field, and Louise Rainer. That's a huge 9021-uh-oh, if you ask me.

The moral: No matter what manages to get your extreme motivation center ramped up in this world, that's what you will need to find in order to stay motivated.

Confident

Luckily, we are born both ignorant and confident. Somehow, though, we manage to mess it all up by getting older and learning just enough to be scared of anything we don't understand 1000 percent. This is where a child's blind faith and the expertise of con-men comes in handy.

> All you need in this life is ignorance and confidence, and then success is sure.
> —*Mark Twain*

Chin-Ning Chu, author of *Thick Face Black Heart* states, "The world has a tendency to accept our own judgment of ourselves. If you exude self-confidence, people will naturally want to let you succeed. Self-doubt creates a perception of incompetence."

What happens as a result is that we are given massive latitude to succeed when we merely demonstrate confidence. This is the second half of the secret used by the con-man Frank Abagnale, Jr., (the first being vocabulary) to successfully impersonate several highly trained professionals throughout his con-man career. The long form of *con-man,* by the way, is *confidence-man!*

Therefore, to ensure that others help us succeed, we need to either have a better estimation of ourselves or have a way of temporarily creating the impression that we do until we actually do. There are a few ways to increase our own estimation of ourselves, and while there are no shortcuts, the reality is that a little regular self-reflection (as with the weekly exercise previously outlined) will go a long way to helping you realize that your estimation of yourself is likely far less generous than it should be.

The most surefire way to boost our own confidence is with a taste of a little success. The key word here is *little.* If we shoot too high and don't nail it right out of the gate, it will have the opposite effect, but if we test ourselves with a goal just outside our comfort zone and nail it, we'll feel capable of more next time. This could be auditioning for the regional play or the school orchestra, losing five pounds, or even finishing this book. Just set a few small goals that are a little beyond your comfort zone, and hit them out of the park!

With nearly twenty years experience in entertainment under my belt, I can tell you that I am infinitely more confident when I walk into a meeting or an audition today than I was when I was starting out. The vast majority of that confidence came in little chunks made up of minor wins along the way.

The Power of *As If*

It wasn't always that way for me at the beginning though, as it may not be for you. The good news is that you can still tap into the power of confidence before you have a lot of it.

> Be careful what you pretend to be because you are what you pretend to be.
> —*Kurt Vonnegut, Jr.*

The first time I encountered the concept of *as if* was while studying the acting philosophy and technique of Sanford Meisner, who is considered to be among the most highly respected acting teachers of our time. If you are interested in acting, I highly recommend his book, *Sanford Meisner, On Acting,* as a must-read. My first and second copy were so dog-eared, highlighted, and beat-up, in fact, that I had to re-buy it three times!

The technique of *as if* as it applies to acting is a simple solution to portraying an emotion of a character even if you can't directly relate to that character's particular situation in your own life. You simply find something that you can relate to and think about that while saying the lines of the character.

So, for example, if the character you're portraying has just lost his mother, but you, the actor, have fortunately never lost a person close to you, you simply replace the image of this terrible loss with something you can relate to: perhaps the memory of burying your childhood dog, or the day you found out that you failed third grade, or being dumped by your true love, anything that has the ability to bring a similar physical and emotional reaction when you think about it. The trigger may be totally different, but the outcome is the same as far as anyone knows, and people will applaud your depth and understanding of this character even though you may not actually have any clue what the character is going through—it's just *as if* you do.

This technique also applies in real life when you need to be confident even though you feel much less so. This is one of the greatest success secrets of some of the most successful people to ever live. Simply substitute the emotion of something you are

An oft-repeated story holds that while shooting *Marathon Man* in 1976, Lawrence Olivier famously quipped to Dustin Hoffman, after witnessing Dustin's "method" acting technique of not sleeping for days and generally becoming a living mess in order to get into character, "Dear boy, it's called acting."

confident about while doing something you aren't, and the world will accept this as your estimation of yourself and offer you all of the same latitude for success anyway!

> Men acquire a particular quality by constantly acting a particular way. You become just by performing just actions . . . brave by performing brave actions.
>
> —*Aristotle*

Fake It 'Til You Make It

Aristotle suggests you can also trigger a new state of being simply by pretending to be that way consistently. Let's say you wake up feeling tired, unmotivated, or irritable, but you have several meetings today and perhaps an audition, all of which require you to come across like an energized, motivated, and charming candidate, which, according to the alarm clock buried in your drywall, is decidedly not how you feel right now. It is, of course, possible to act *as if* you're energized, motivated, charming, even though you don't feel it.

This was radically demonstrated in a study at UC Berkeley, cited by Anthony Robbins on his CD *Get the Edge.* Researchers instructed participants who were clinically depressed to stand in front of a mirror for twenty minutes a day, for four straight weeks, and smile—from ear to ear. The participants were told to stand with their shoulders back and breathe fully. After only four weeks of doing this daily, most of the participants did not need their antidepressant medications anymore.

That is the power of acting *as if!* We've all seen people who are almost annoyingly good at this. It could be cold and raining, but they're walking around like it's the most beautiful spring day on earth. Some may dismiss them as crazy, but to me if it's a kind of crazy I can use to my benefit, then go ahead and call me crazy!

Take It from the Donald

In Donald Trump's book *Think Big and Kick Ass,* "The Donald" admits to using this powerful technique regularly. Something as simple as wearing thousand-dollar suits (even when he was broke) and carrying a huge wad of cash in his pocket gave him the feeling of importance, power, and control while building his real estate empire from scratch.

Acting *as if* has a magical way of becoming reality. Not only do other people start to see us as the success we're pretending to be, but most importantly, we start to see ourselves that way too.

Some of the greatest actors of all time will tell you that they do not ever truly get into character until they are in full costume. It's one reason that I *never* audition for a role (or even any non-acting job!) without dressing for it in some way!

To audition for the role of "Number 2" in *Austin Powers in Goldmember* (the character originated by Robert Wagner in the first *Austin Powers* and then played by Rob Lowe in the second film), I went to Macy's and bought a five-hundred-dollar suit and to a dime store to get an eye patch to wear to the audition.

It's not just that I don't trust the imaginations of casting directors (I don't), but it's because it made me *feel* more like the character, which helped me act more like the character. Incidentally, I kept the receipt and returned the suit after I got the job . . . always keep the receipt!

Just think of the way wearing a tuxedo or a nice dress makes you feel different from the everyday. How about the time you got out of a limo at a restaurant, or the way you felt driving a rented sports car? People buy and use these "superficial" things because they make them feel a certain way—and if they *feel* confident, that makes them confident. It's another prime example of the strategic use of props!

In the end, if Chu is right that "the world has a tendency to accept our own judgment of ourselves," then people who exude confidence will always win a heck of a lot more than people who don't! So act *as if* you're confident today and see what happens.

There is a second use of this technique that you can apply to any situation where you must do something or make a decision but have no personal reference from experience what that action or decision should be. Simply imagining what someone you admire would do in this situation takes your own emotion out of it and allows you to make decisions and do things *as if* you were Donald Trump, Madonna, Oprah, Jesus, Harrison Ford . . . you get the point. It's a simple twist, but it really works!

> People respond well to people who are sure of what they want.
> —*Anna Wintour, editor in chief of Vogue*

Decisive

As I have hopefully already made clear, you have to know what you want in life, and specifically what you want in terms of your career in order to get it. But then you need to *decide* to do it. Your vocabulary from now on should support this, in much the same way I had decided to do the things I set out to do in 1995 when I moved to New York, as opposed to "trying" to do them.

Forget about the "What if it doesn't happens" or the "I'm not sure I cans," because one thing that successful artists know is that these thoughts are the thoughts of those who *don't do it.* When they feel these things as all humans do, they have learned to acknowledge the feeling but let it go quickly.

So how do you *decide* to do something? It's very simple; you first decide to decide, and then you start taking action on that decision immediately.

Self-described life coach and world-famous inspirational speaker Anthony Robbins likes to say, "I never leave the site of a decision without first taking action." He also credits decisiveness with being one of the most powerful success tools available to everyone. In *Awaken the Giant Within,* one of the best-selling self-improvement books of all time, he points out that the three decisions that control your destiny are:

1. Your decisions about what to focus on.

2. Your decisions about what things mean to you.

3. Your decisions about what to do to create the results you desire.

We already have a good idea of what to focus on (chapter 5), and the way we determine meaning for ourselves is also determined by the questions we ask (chapter 7), but this last critical distinction, as Anthony points out, speaks to the actions we take. And the very first action is the decision itself.

Decisiveness is actually like any other muscle in our bodies: it only becomes strong when we train it. To harness the power of decisiveness, you will have to start small, and do *a lot* of repetitions. Before long, you'll be capable of easily making a huge decision with little effort.

In practice, this means no longer saying things like, "I don't care, what are you in the mood for?" or "It doesn't matter to me."

It should matter to you, a lot.

We tend to operate throughout most of our day on habit, so even if it seems petty to be very decisive about what restaurant to eat at this afternoon, by not making the decision affirmatively and actively, you are only letting your "decision muscles" atrophy. Now obviously this doesn't mean we need to drag our friends to only the places we want to go, but it does mean that we have to learn—or relearn—how to express these desires as a habit each time, especially expressing these desires to ourselves.

This was never my strong suit; I was raised to put others' needs ahead of my own, but once I realized that most of the successful people I was studying used their ability to decide and decide quickly and affirmatively to their advantage, I knew I had to put myself on a strict decision workout, and that began with the seemingly petty stuff. Before long, I was managing big decisions like what I was going to do with my life, and the next thing I knew I found myself somewhere outside Alabama in a beat up Ford Tempo, headed to New York City, on a mission.

Insatiable

As I mentioned in chapter 3, I believe that if it is ever proven that a single gene can be isolated to determine success, it will be the gene that determines drive. And to have drive, you need to have an insatiable hunger for that thing that you want most in life.

Where does hunger come from? Anywhere. You just have to want something badly enough that you will stop at nothing to get it. Something that will take you outside your comfort zone, and force you to take massive action, and risk everything in order to get it.

I'm no psychologist, but this sounds a lot like the same frame of mind you'd imagine people on the brink of survival having—people who have done unimaginable things in order to simply live one more day or provide for their families.

Since I obviously would never wish such circumstances on anyone, I would suggest that most people who have displayed an insatiable drive to succeed and who were not also survivors of tremendous circumstance likely found their drive through being inspired by others.

I personally have always found inspiration in biographies, especially ones that became great films. The movie *The Pursuit of Happyness,* the true story of Chris Gardner, a homeless father who becomes a stockbroker in order to provide for his family, is just such an inspirational story. Or *Rudy,* the true story of Daniel "Rudy" Ruettiger, who overcame significant obstacles including poor grades, small size, and lacking any discernable natural talent to not only gain acceptance to Notre Dame, one of the best universities in the country, but to play football for them as well! Even fiction works! How many people do you think left the movie *Rocky* ready to take on the world?

Sometimes, though, the best way to get hungry is to back off the food. Simply creating a situation for yourself, even if it's only in your head, where it feels like success is the only alternative to starving to death, can be a powerful motivator.

Whatever makes you perpetually hungry for success—find it. It will likely require searching, as it will be something different for everyone.

Join the Club

One place to find insatiability is in groups of other people who share this trait. If you've ever been around a group of people who seem to over-achieve constantly, you know how infectious it is. You just seem to start doing and wanting the same things almost as if by osmosis.

It's no surprise that such a high percentage of the cast of the 1990s TV show *The All-New Mickey Mouse Club,* many of them friends, went on to become superstars in their own right. I'm referring to Grammy Award–winning singers Justin Timberlake, Britney Spears, Christina Aguilera, and J. C. Chasez, as well as Golden Globe–winning actress Kerri Russell and Academy Award–nominated actor Ryan Gosling.

It's not just a coincidence that such a high percentage of kids from such a small group went on to find that amount of success. Their bar was set higher by competing, to some degree, with each other and by a desire to become like the people they themselves idolized.

The two key components of becoming insatiable are studying those who succeeded on a level unimaginable to most and surrounding yourself by people who do the same.

Self-Reflective

Being self-reflective is very difficult for many of us because, frankly, ignorance can be bliss. Thankfully, most of us have a conscience, but we also figure out early on that if we don't *know* that something needs changing or improving, then we won't feel compelled to do anything about it by that very same conscience. This is the most destructive form of laziness, in my opinion.

The most successful artists in this industry are the ones who not only have a very strong compulsion to do things better, but they are the opposite of most average people in that they are constantly seeking ways to change and improve. In other words, they are self-reflective and are not lazy.

To better describe self-reflection, I've often made the comparison to super-computers. In its simplest form, the best computer in the world is the one that analyzes the most data the fastest, then quickly discards useless information so that it can further analyze relevant information, in order to find the absolute best solution in the least amount of time.

To become a superstar requires the desire to act like a super-computer, and to do this you need to be and/or become a self-reflective person in the first place. In other words, you have to be willing to not be ignorant. And this is a conscious choice.

This means actually taking time to reflect—daily, weekly, monthly, and annually—on what's working and what's not. It means discarding what's not working and devising a new plan when necessary. It's that simple. Once you've decided to not be ignorant, basic human nature takes over and propels you forward.

I've spelled out a weekly exercise already, but to take your success rate up a notch, start doing that same exercise daily, then put it on your calendar to ask the broader question once a month. Just make it part of your higher standards to do so.

I recommend that once a year you—literally—take a vacation. Leave town; go somewhere away from the industry, and spend a full week or so reflecting on the single question: How did I do this year, and what can I do better? Getting out of the old environment really helps stir up possibilities and helps get back in touch with why you're doing this in the first place. It's a way of gaining perspective.

It also helps to reward yourself annually with a vacation for all of the sacrifice you had to make in order to pursue your dreams!

Rule 7: Seek the six-pack of becoming extremely creative, self-motivated, confident, decisive, insatiable, and self-reflective in not just the show side, but also the business side of show business. Until those words best describe you, fake it till you make it by acting *as if* you already are those things.

Instinct: The Lost Art and the Artist's Domain

The intellect has little to do on the road to discovery. There comes a leap in consciousness, call it intuition or what you will, and the solution comes to you and you don't know why.

—ALBERT EINSTEIN

It's been said that the main difference between human beings and animals is our ability to reason. As humans, we not only value our ability to reason, but in many ways we worship reason with every difficult decision we make. For example: Let's think this through (pros and cons). What do you think (opposing views)? I need more details first (postponement). Yes, these are valuable tools, but for far too many of us, the pendulum of reason has swung so far to the side of dependence that we have become our own worst enemy.

We've all been guilty of favoring the safe advice over our own inner voice, whether it was being urged to study the—more respectable—viola in middle school when guitar was what really turned you on (as in my case), playing a sport you hated for the same reason, going to a college that your parents insisted was best for you but made your heart sink, then studying a "safe" subject to prepare you for a "safe" job you hate, because that's what you thought society expected of you.

If the economic meltdown of 2007 has taught us anything, it's that safe doesn't exist anymore, good advice is, more often than not and at best, uninformed opinion, and most of what that little voice inside our head was saying all along was actually dead on!

Be Wary of Group-Think

One of the biggest obstacles you will surely face in the entertainment industry is the phenomenon known as group-think. Hundreds of studies have shown that people will routinely choose an option they *know* to be incorrect, just because everyone else has chosen it. We reason that even though our instincts tell us to choose one thing, there must be a valid reason everyone else is choosing the other, and away we go like lemmings over the cliff.

As an artist, this will prevent you from going where you really need to go in order to find success, which is very often in the exact opposite direction.

It is likely, since you're reading a book about breaking into and thriving in the entertainment industry, that you're already ignoring the loudest, even if well-intentioned, advice givers, who are telling you that success in this business is a pipe dream and a giant gamble, and you should just make it a hobby. That was the advice that kept me on the "safe" path until I was twenty-three. I've heard it all, and so has everyone who ever succeeded in this field and, like me, they went after their dreams anyway, despite advice to the contrary.

This chapter is not about the safe advice from your parents, guidance counselor, or friends. (I'm going to assume that after reading chapter 3, Is This For You?, you've made an informed decision to follow your dream despite any of these warnings.)

This is about the bad advice you'll be getting from people inside the entertainment industry, which can often be just as bad and, in some cases, worse.

Those who scream the loudest know the least.

The wisdom of this proverb is that there is no natural motivation to announce things we already know to be absolutely true. For example, I know brushing my teeth is a good idea, but I don't feel compelled to go out every day and announce it on the street corner. The fact is that most of the advice you'll hear will come from people not qualified to give it, and when we hear someone offering loud or unsolicited advice, it's usually a case of them trying to convince themselves of the idea for a particular reason that has no significant bearing on our own personal reality.

And since Madonna probably won't be calling you up anytime soon to give you a few pointers on the recording industry, a great question you're likely asking yourself is: Well then, who should I listen to? The answer is simple: yourself.

In fact, when I would meet people for the first time in New York, I would often avoid telling them my career aspirations simply to avoid having to endure their likely uninformed opinion about them. I figured I wouldn't have to overcome bad advice I never heard! If, and only if, they turned out to be a supportive ally with access to useful and critical information, I would let them in on my plan. I didn't want anyone messing with my head and affecting my instincts!

Instincts Combine Everything You Have Ever Known to Be True into One Map

The antidote to bad advice goes like this: seek out as much information as you can from the best sources out there, and then simply go with your instinct when making important decisions.

This is a component of self-reliance and a skill that becomes a trait when trained. The moments when you listen to your instinct and it turns out to be 100 percent correct—despite the loud cries in opposition—are the moments you begin to become the person most likely to succeed. Stack several of these moments together and you'll find that your confidence will grow exponentially and you'll be able to more efficiently dissect all of the information coming at you into one of three categories: garbage, useful, and worth exploring further.

In my career, my instincts took me to New York City, even though many tried to convince me to go to LA. I somehow just knew my energetic personality would have been swallowed whole in LA by the laid-back pace. I thrived in New York.

My instinct told me there was a better route to finding an agent than what everyone else was doing.

My instinct told me that acting classes and voice lessons were only a means to get a job, not a place to get comfortable like most of my colleagues around me. Those same instincts told me to quit a particular acting class the second my teacher tried to convince me not to audition for work or seek an agent until *she* said I was ready! I booked a commercial a day later that made me 150K that year. I guess I was ready after all.

My instinct told me to get a subsistence job that wouldn't become a social life, so that I'd always remain motivated to succeed.

My instinct told me to save money, to not buy a lot of flashy stuff in 1998, even when I was making quite a bit of money and while many other successful actors around me spent money like it was growing on trees. When my first streak ended, this instinct allowed me spend my time looking for my next job instead of standing behind a coffee shop counter.

This list could go on and on, but the one thread that penetrates each one of these scenarios is that I listened to what the voice inside my head was telling me, despite the fact that everyone around me was often telling me and doing the opposite. I now know that most of them were lemmings headed off the cliff.

Was this always easy? NO! Groupthink is a freakishly powerful phenomenon, but it has to be overcome with practice. The first step, of course, is recognizing it. Be careful, though: don't just do something different for the sake of being different. That's equally as dangerous.

At the point of any critical decision, I have personally always relied on that uneasy feeling in my gut that said, "Wait a minute, something's off here." Are these other folks doing something smart or are they missing the opportunity that I think I see?" When my instinct answers, I leap.

What does your gut tell you? Start listening!

Rule 8: Learn to depend on your instinct and be wary of group-think and well-intentioned "advice" in order to find a better, faster, and more reliable way to get to where you're going.

Integrity

I NTEGRITY CAN BE defined as *the quality of being honest and having strong moral principles; moral uprightness.* Want to stand out in this industry? Have integrity. Make this central to your life and career, and it will make you relatively unique in show business and very desirable to hire.

There's no upside to having a bad or even somewhat tarnished reputation, only an extra obstacle to overcome each time you want a job and/or want to keep one.

Believe me, I'm not interested in chastising fallen celebrities or even pointing out all of the ways this industry turns its head to abuses, excesses, and depravity. This is also not about the way tabloids celebrate controversy. Yes, some stars always seem to weather tabloid storms of their own creation. I have known a few of them, and trust me when I tell you that they are miserable and most often extremely sick people. Ultimately though, the list of famous people who have lost their money, career, and respect is as long as it is sad.

The simple point here is that being a person of integrity not only gives you a distinct advantage in this industry, but it is also the single largest determining factor in whether or not you will enjoy a long and fulfilling career once you break in.

Only you can establish exactly what integrity means to you, and it is absolutely critical that you take the time to sit down and define it for yourself. You need to clearly identify your core values. If you don't, they will probably be handed to you by default, whether you approve or not.

> Principles only mean something if you stick by them when they're inconvenient.
>
> —FROM THE FILM *THE CONTENDER*, BY ROD LURIE

I distinctly remember one of the few times in my life when someone openly questioned my integrity. That particular experience was so awful and so eye-opening that I have never forgotten it, and it prompted a big turning point in my life. As a sophomore in college, I was mistakenly accused of something I hadn't done by an employer. Although my boss soon realized that his accusation was false and retracted it, the very idea that my reputation as a person of integrity could be so easily questioned in the first place horrified me. I realized at that moment that I hadn't taken the time to think about whether I was projecting a value system I could be proud of. Instead, I had always been far more concerned with trying to be funny or clever, and in hindsight, that likely led to the confusion.

I spent the next few weeks searching my soul for the exact values that I wanted to be admired for possessing. I took Stephen Covey's advice and started with my own funeral and identified exactly what it was that I wanted to be said about me when I was gone. I also made the choice that instead of being insulted and angry about being falsely accused, I would decide to take a cue from it and make sure that from that moment on, I'd always be given the benefit of the doubt in *any* situation based on my overtly obvious character.

Although I was admittedly mad at the time, I'm eternally grateful for this experience. By the time I hit New York a few years later, I had already made it my trademark to be known as a man of integrity, and I did this with my actions, not my words.

Through my actions, I became known as a guy who always shows up earlier, works harder, and leaves later than most.

I'm nothing if not a man of my word, regardless of whether keeping my word is convenient to me or not. Often, standing by commitments has meant making very large personal sacrifices, but I do it anyway.

I treat everyone with extreme courtesy. I never take advantage of anyone or anything just because I can, and above all, I earn, ounce for ounce, everything I receive honestly, including respect, or else I don't take it.

I have accountability. I take full responsibility for my mistakes regardless of how embarrassing they might be.

To this day, I believe that the highest compliment I can receive is someone pointing out my integrity. I am far from perfect, and these things are not always easy. I make mistakes and I occasionally fall short, but I try every day to live up to those values I decided are important to me, and it has paid off for me in spades.

Just as people want to hire the most skilled person, people first and foremost want to work with people they can trust and rely on. I've been hired for many jobs simply because I was the more reliable candidate, though not necessarily the most skilled or naturally talented choice. All the skill and talent in the world doesn't matter one bit if that person doesn't show up or is disruptive, difficult, or unreliable!

I've seen extremely gifted people simply not get hired for another job again after a show we both worked on has ended. Even after breaking in, one of the toughest things to do, their career ended abruptly based entirely on the negative reputation they created for themselves once they got a shot. Worse, I've seen people get fired from great jobs, dream jobs, because they lacked integrity.

In this business, being branded as a problem, especially the kind that gets you fired, does not happen quietly. People find out. And if you thought breaking in was tough, try breaking *back in* when everyone is suddenly predisposed to not trust or like you!

The Diva Myth

The first people to be described as divas were in the world of opera, and the word was originally used in a positive way to denote a woman of outstanding talent. However, it has lately also taken on a decidedly negative connotation. UrbanDictionary.com defines *diva* as a bitchy woman who must have her way exactly, or no way at all. She is often rude and belittles people, believing that everyone is beneath her, and she thinks that she is so much more loved than what she really is. Divas are selfish, spoiled, and overly dramatic.

Even so, earning the title of "diva" is still something many people aspire to. The assumption is that divas are so talented they can behave any way they want to without any consequences. But just ask yourself . . . why would you want to?

What I all too often end up seeing as a result are people—men and women—incorrectly using the *as if* technique in a way that virtually guarantees failure down the road. They act *as if* they are better than anyone around them, and as a result the people around them simply desire to prove them wrong, no matter how talented they really are. It's just human nature.

Instead of people assuming someone like this is talented based on self-confidence and therefore wanting to help them succeed (the correct usage of *as if*), they'll be offended by this "I'm better than you" attitude and will do whatever they can to knock the person back down to earth.

Once again, the big question ultimately is: why set up more obstacles for yourself this way? Truly talented and hardworking people don't need to rub it in everyone's face—they have applause, paychecks, and more job offers as proof of their worth.

Take my word on this: project genuine humility at all times, and above all, don't be a diva!

Rule 9: Make being a person of integrity and humility your trademark and don't be a diva.

PART IV

SKILLS

As I have already stated, in the business of entertainment you are many things: an entrepreneur, a business owner, a salesperson, and an artist (i.e., the product you're selling), and you are those things in that exact order of importance! This means that you have to deal with several variables that your average company employee may never have to think twice about. This requires mastering a few key skills, skills that often determine the difference between being an artist and being a working artist.

The most obvious difference between artists and most other trade professions is that work itself can be fleeting and extremely fickle—even for artists who are already established and sometimes even very famous. This factor alone will require you to master the art of money management and emotional management.

Since *you* are also the product that you are selling, you need to treat yourself as a product by managing your image like any other brand, as well as learning how to sell yourself effectively.

If you ask anyone who's had success in any form of sales: What's the most important skill that the profession requires? They'll tell you it's networking, and not the kind of networking that begins and ends at "friending" someone on a social media site either. The skill of sales-networking requires the *sun-up to sundown, banging on doors, sending out thank you cards, flying across the country for face-to-face time* type of networking that terrifies most people. Since you're not out to be like most people, here's what you need to know.

Get Rich and Stay Rich: Five Rules to Live By Now

BEING BROKE SUCKS. Being famous and broke sucks even more, and being famously broke is by far the worst. In the first instance, you're merely like most of the world.

By the time you're famous from contributing to some aspect of entertainment in a bankable way, you may not be ridiculously wealthy—most are not—but you've probably at least made enough money to be considered somewhat financially successful. But losing something you once had always seems to sting a lot more than to have never had it in the first place.

The last category, the MC Hammers of the world, get all the above-mentioned anguish plus the humiliation of being as famous for their financial blunders as they are for their artistry.

Perhaps the most important thing to know about finances with regard to the entertainment industry is this:

Planning, saving, and investing will require almost as much of your time and focus as your actual career if you ever hope to become financially free.

What do I mean by *financially free*? I mean nothing short of creating the kind of self-perpetuating wealth through saving and investing that allows you to work or not work, as you please, forever. The kind of wealth that allows you to pick and choose only the most attractive jobs, the most inspiring or risky jobs, that you otherwise would never be able to wait for or risk taking if you were constantly worrying about paying your next bills.

And here's another truth that may surprise you: You do not need to become a superstar, raking in millions per picture or album, in order to have this become your reality! I know of several full-time entertainers that I bet you've never heard of who have found total financial freedom. These people religiously followed the five rules I will spell out and made learning about smart investing (not merely handing your money over to a stockbroker and praying) a second job. More accurately, they made it a second obsession.

I once worked with an on-again and off-again Broadway dancer who now owns an apartment building in New York City that earns her, besides the tax advantages, enough income to never have to work again. Of course she still does work, but only on her terms! This is a woman who never made more than $150,000 in a good year (not a lot by New York City standards)!

I have several friends who make their living doing nothing but TV commercials who also never have to work again but do it because they love it. They were able to do this simply because they learned how to create wealth by creating assets that put money in their pocket whether they're working or not.

The truth is that surviving and thriving financially in the entertainment industry doesn't actually require a special set of rules. The rules are the same for everyone, and they are the very same rules, in fact, that most people in the world likely wished they had followed before the Great Recession of 2007!

Surviving and thriving in entertainment does, however, require far greater discipline in adhering strictly to the rules and always operating within only the smallest margins of risk. I call it being "unconventionally" financially responsible. This means taking all of the time-tested financial common sense and living by it religiously without straying.

In a career that ebbs and flows as much as entertainment does, it doesn't matter how talented or lucky you feel now or become in the future. This is an industry in which you will almost always have less stability (note that I did not say less money) than almost any other career out there and you can be sure that things *will* change. Just ask MC Hammer, who declared bankruptcy with $13 million in debt, or Nicolas Cage, who went bankrupt at the height of his fame and owed more than $6 million in back taxes! They're just two of a huge list of celebrities who went broke even after achieving superstardom. Some bounced back; many did not.

Here's a few others that may surprise you:

- Michael Jackson died on June 25, 2009, with $400 million in debt.
- Burt Reynolds filed for bankruptcy in 1996 with more than $11 million in debt.
- Kim Basinger filed for bankruptcy in 1993 with $8 million in debt.
- Toni Braxton filed for bankruptcy in 1998 with almost $4 million in debt.
- Jerry Lee Lewis filed for bankruptcy in 1975 with $3 million of debt.
- Larry King filed for bankruptcy in 1978 with $352,000 in debt.

I personally have been broke, and I have also been famous and almost-broke as a result of stretching a few of the following five rules that I now adhere to unfailingly. What has saved me from true embarrassment, however—from the "famously broke" type of embarrassment—was the fact that, even with all of my mistakes, I never violated money rule number one, which is:

Live BENEATH your means.

Short of being handed wealth, the only way to find financial freedom in this business is to live beneath your means . . . period. Even the idea of living *within* your means is slated for far more stable careers.

Yes, entertainment can and hopefully will pay big for you, but it almost never does so consistently, and especially not at first. As demonstrated above, there are hundreds of stories of great and seemingly impenetrable careers being penetrated by outside circumstances that no one saw coming. The way to avoid this is very simple:

No matter what you make in income, spend less.

In order to one day have the kind of freedom to pick and choose work without having to consider the financial element (aka financial freedom) you should consider taking this idea one step further:

When you start to make more income, simply continue spending about the same amount each month as you did before you had it.

This should be your rule at least until your investment income alone is generating enough money to live on. I'll cover investments in a minute, but for now, any and all extra cash should be earmarked for one of three categories: emergency savings, investing, and insurance.

For example, let's say you make and spend $1000 a month bartending. Then all of a sudden you get a big break and find yourself making $40,000 a month. Simply continue to spend $1000 a month and allocate the extra $39,000 a month (or whatever is left over after taxes) toward each of the three categories above.

If you can maintain this kind of discipline until your investments earn you at least $1000 a month on their own, then you'll never have to worry about the basics again!

If you can maintain it just a little bit longer, then you will very quickly be able to increase your lifestyle in a permanent way! It really is that simple.

The reality at play here is that if you never become accustomed to a higher lifestyle in the meantime, you'll never find yourself missing it, which is a lot easier than giving up a nice lifestyle down the road.

All the extra money you're suddenly making will become one hell of a safety net, which—I can tell you from experience—could save your career and, more importantly, your sanity one day.

I'm not saying that you should never treat yourself to anything nice as a reward for your work and sacrifice; in fact I suggest you do treat yourself reasonably with each big win. But the more you can keep your lifestyle in check, the better off you will be until the day comes when you are truly financially capable of living the lifestyle of the rich and famous . . . permanently.

A Big Myth of the Rich and Famous

Ironically, many of the rich and famous you see are not really rich; most of their supposed "wealth" is actually built on credit and, sadly for some, it will all come crashing down on them eventually, as the world watches through the tabloids. Worse than that, the vast majority of the rich and famous will only be famous for a little while. Broke and no one cares is a huge price to pay for a few minutes of false glamour. After all, as Eric Clapton pointed out, "Nobody knows you when you're down and out. In your pocket, not one penny, and as for friends, you don't have any."

If It Could Happen to Me . . .

Hopefully the following true story of my first experience transitioning from broke bartender to cash-flush actor will illustrate how small the margins are for entertainers, even when we more or less follow the rules!

By 1998, three and a half years after I arrived in New York City, I had a steady bartending job and was starting to gain some momentum in the entertainment world. From the day I had moved to New York, I had figured out a way to live on exactly $1000 a month, which included rent, health insurance, and a little food.

With my ability to consistently make at least $1200 a month bartending, I saved no less than $200 monthly.

When I intermittently made more than $1200 a month with the entertainment jobs, I would save exactly that much more.

By 1998, I had saved $12,000, which included putting $2000 per year into my IRA ($6000 total) and another $6000 saved as an emergency fund, which I ended up using to immediately pay the exorbitant entry fee into the three main actors' unions: AEA (Actor's Equity Association), AFTRA (the American Federation of Television and Radio Artists), and SAG (the Screen Actors Guild) when I was forced to do so in order to keep working. As you may know or will hopefully find out soon, they will require you to join after you work a certain number of union jobs, and it's not cheap!

Then I hit pay dirt. I booked a small role in the major motion picture *Shaft Returns,* starring Samuel Jackson, and the lead role in MTV's first made-for-TV movie, *2GE+HER,* which spawned its own TV series of the same name. In a single day, I went from making $1200 a month to around $40,000 a month, which lasted for about two years.

Even when I moved out to LA to accommodate the shooting schedule for *2GE+HER,* my expenses (including a used Jeep I paid cash for) only went up about $100 a month.

Everything else I earned, every penny, I was banking. And that was a good thing too. Three things happened in the year 2000 that easily could have derailed me financially. It was like a perfect storm.

The first was that my bread and butter show, *2GE+HER,* was cancelled shortly after my good friend and fellow cast member Michael Cuccione passed away after a long battle with cancer.

The second was a series of entertainment union strikes that

occurred around the same time, which effectively stalled most new productions for a year. In anticipation of the strikes, the studios and networks had stockpiled extra productions that were filled with actors who were available for work while I was still shooting *2GE+HER;* in other words, while I was unavailable.

In 2000, I was out of a job, and my on-screen caché as a rising actor cooled while the unions and studios duked it out for the better part of a year. Even when the battle was over, there was such a large stockpile of "new" shows that very few opportunities for actors like myself remained for still another year or so to come.

Just like that, I became a has-been.

Financially, this wasn't a problem for me, because I had banked almost a half million dollars and—since I'd never increased my lifestyle—I had very few expenses.

Then the third thing, the rogue wave, hit. With all that time on my hands, I decided I should look into investing this huge pile of money so that I would never have to worry about money again. Remember the dot-com bubble? The bubble burst just two weeks after I had slid nearly all of my money over and into the "expert" hands of a financial advisor from the now-defunct financial services firm Lehman Brothers. Are you laughing yet?

Luckily, I took my financial reigns back just in time to rescue about a hundred thousand of the half million.

Rescuing a mere $100,000 from certain extinction allowed me just enough time (three years to be exact) to reinvent my career and become the host of the Emmy-nominated home makeover show *While You Were Out* on the Learning Channel (TLC). My comeback took three years, and I had managed to land on one of the highest-rated cable networks at the time without ever having to bartend a single day in between, but not before learning a very valuable lesson, which is:

Money Rule #2: No one should ever control your money but you.

A whole book could be written (and many I'm sure have) on why entertainers and professional athletes seem to fall prey, more often than others, to unscrupulous money managers. The bottom line is that the only way to protect yourself from really bad choices is to become educated on basic finances and accounting, carefully surround yourself by trusted advisors (not just popular ones—hello, Bernie Madoff!), and always be the final decision-maker on everything related to your money. You have to remain in the loop!

This may sound like common sense, but the path to financial destruction is riddled with the classic excuses: "I'm an artist, not a numbers person. I don't have time. They're experts at what they do, not me," and on and on. Get lazy here, and you will get taken, I promise you. Just ask Kevin Bacon and Kyra Sedgwick, who invested with Bernie Madoff. Returns that are too good to be true are usually just that!

I made the mistake of confusing the fancy financial speak of an "expert" investment advisor with intelligence and honesty. In hindsight, not one word of what he had to say was sound or, frankly, easy to understand. He was certainly not providing financial advice that had my best interests in mind.

As a result, I trusted him to invest almost all of my money right into dot-com stocks, laughably, only two weeks before the bubble burst. He made off with a small fortune in trade commissions and I lost 300K almost overnight. He may have even actually believed he would make me a lot of money but the end result was the same. The reward system he was operating in rewarded him on the volume of trades, not intelligent decisions, which I found out later. Simply put, I blew it by not doing my homework.

Hindsight being 20/20, I would have been far better off diversifying into money market funds and bonds and learning to create streams of passive income, such as with rental real estate, but again, in the end I only had myself to blame.

Despite how much we like to blame the bottom feeders for

our financial downfalls, the reality is that it doesn't take a Bernie Madoff or executives at Enron or AIG to squander fortunes. It does, however, almost always involve laziness on the part of the investor. Do your due diligence, and you'll be laughing when the next tsunami comes. The good news is that this is relatively easy to do just by picking up a few good books on investing and finances (some of my favorites are listed in the resources section in the back of this book).

So how do you find a good advisor? The first path is through effective networking, which we'll get to shortly. Regardless of who you consult, there is one very simple test I apply when interviewing prospective advisors, and something I do continuously with the one I'm currently using to make sure I'm still getting the best and most up-to-date wisdom. If an advisor cannot explain to me exactly what his or her strategy is and how he or she operates so that I can understand it clearly, I walk.

Of course I do my own research ahead of time so I have an idea of what kind of strategies I'm comfortable with, and what kind of reputation and track record the person has, but any financial advisor who cannot, or will not, translate the financial world into everyday, common-sense language for a client is, in my opinion, either socially impaired (not good), just lazy (also not good), or hiding something (definitely not good).

Today, my advisor of more than a decade specializes in working with entertainment clients—this person was recommended to me by a trusted friend and by my long-time agent. As much as I trust him, however, I still constantly read books on money and investing, and I track changes in the economy in order to make sure that when a particular investment strategy is recommended, I understand exactly why. And I don't always agree.

Money Rule #3: Credit is not your friend.

Entertainment careers that are stable sources of income are rare to nonexistent, which means that we absolutely cannot count on being able to pay off debts in the future. There are too many variables outside of our control, no matter how secure we might feel about things today.

As a result of this, there is absolutely no logical argument for carrying debt. The big trap is when you attempt to live like a "normal person" with a relatively stable job and buy things the way they do, i.e. on credit. Remember, even the normal people got called out in the financial meltdown of 2007! As the legendary investor, Warren Buffet says, you find out who's skinny dipping when the tide goes out!

In fact, even while I was living way below my means, I got caught on this one as well, because I stretched the rules just a hair. Although I have never in my life spent a dime on a credit card that was not paid off in full every month, I did manage to fall prey to the lure and convenience of mortgage credit.

> Your home is not an asset, it's a liability. An asset is something that puts money in your pocket. A liability is something that takes money out of your pocket. When you buy a home to live in that you pay for with a home loan, it's taking money out of your pocket and putting it into a banker's!
>
> —ROBERT KIYOSAKI, AUTHOR, SPEAKER, ENTREPRENEUR, ZILLIONAIRE

The Embarrassing Lesson

After refilling my coffers with four years of hosting home makeover shows, I purchased a house with my wife that I could have paid for in cash had I liquidated a large chunk of my savings and investments.

I felt it was a safe, conservative move, and as far as most conventional thinking was concerned, it was . . . until another perfect storm erupted. This time it started with our house burning down. While insurance covered some of it, I had found out the hard way that I had mistakenly underinsured the house, an extremely common mistake, it turns out.

At the same time, my mother's cancer returned. Distracted and devastated on two fronts, as well as being stretched too thin, I had no energy left to go out and nurture my career the way I otherwise would have.

Finally, on the heels of rebuilding the house and my mother losing her battle with cancer the following year, my wife and I decided to move to Nashville in 2006 to be closer to family. We did what was extremely common back then and put a handsome nonrefundable deposit down on a preconstruction property in Nashville, giving us a full year and a half to sell our newly rebuilt house in New York.

This did not go as hoped. Even after lowering the price to far below market, we were unable to sell the house, yet we were forced to close on the Nashville condo to keep from losing the massive deposit we had so confidently laid out. Then the housing market *really* collapsed, and we were now officially stuck with two homes, one of which was now worth far less than what we had paid for it three years earlier.

Needless to say, even though we thought we were being conservative and careful with credit, not adhering to the basic financial rules—religiously—came back to bite me. Luckily, I had adhered strictly to the first rule of living beneath my means, as I always have, and I was able to put enough away to survive being unemployed with multiple mortgages for another three years without again having to bartend or do anything other than concentrate on reinventing my career for a second time.

Instead of curling up and feeling sorry for myself, I reflected on my mistakes and managed to learn a very valuable lesson the hard way. Never buy on credit!

I will never buy a house to live in with a loan again. I bought the one I'm living in now with cash, and I feel unbelievably relaxed these days. I continue to only buy used cars and again, only pay in cash. My new rule (and one I should've been living by all along) is: If I can't pay for something in full, I don't need it . . . yet.

I even bought my airplane with cash. I was able to do this not only through the three money rules already listed, but also by living money rule #4; which also happens to be the first rule of investing for security and prosperity:

Money Rule #4: Learn how to turn regular income into passive income, and create passive income out of thin air.

Every crisis has a silver lining. For me it was being stuck with two homes to pay for. I immediately seized an opportunity to rent one out and by default became a real estate investor. I now own four rental properties that provide passive income whether I'm awake or sleeping. By the time you read this I'll probably own at least double that amount.

One of the inspirations I had to create real estate "lemonade" from my lemony situation came from reading books by a man named Robert Kiyosaki. His best-selling book *Rich Dad Poor Dad* changed the way I viewed money and investing. I have since adopted strict adherence to two of Kiyosaki's key principles, both of which center around creating passive income: assets that will make money while you sleep!

Two Key Rich Dad Principles

1. Invest in passive-income-generating assets with earned income. For me, with my architecture training and construction experience, this has meant buying rental properties that make money while I sleep. (See the appendix for several additional titles that can help you learn to do this too!)
2. *Create* passive income instruments. In other words; invent things that can be licensed indefinitely such as: songs, books, TV shows, movies, how-to videos, the next Sham Wow, etc.

I realized that I may not be able to audition for entertainment jobs forever, and I might even lose interest in them eventually, so I decided to figure out the best ways to have my creativity and my saved money work for me.

You don't need to invent the next iPod, either. As an entertainer, depending on your specific expertise, there are several ways to create passive income without buying real estate or stocks that pay dividends with the money you've already made.

Royalties from writing songs, residuals from working on union films and television, creating a popular YouTube channel, dance instruction videos—any instruction videos—or writing a book are just a few examples of ways to tap your creativity and to license it indefinitely for profit.

Why You Have to Branch Out

This industry is changing fast, and it's not hard to imagine a day soon when few, if any, jobs on television and film will pay residuals like they used to. This is already happening as cable TV is taking over network (union-controlled) broadcasting television, and as it becomes increasingly difficult if not impossible to prevent the pirating of all kinds of entertainment online.

For example, I don't get paid every time one of almost three hundred episodes of *While You Were Out* airs, since it fell under a cable (non-union) contract, but to this day I am still receiving checks every time my episodes of *JAG* or *DAG* air (network television) or my two Screen Actors Guild (SAG) films, *Shaft Returns* and *Austin Powers in Goldmember,* run on TV or in theatres anywhere in the world.

Incidentally, the only reason I still see any money from the combined 1 million copies of the two 2GE+HER albums sold is because I cowrote one of the songs on the first album, making my contribution fall under the jurisdiction of the songwriter's performing rights organization ASCAP, of which I am a member. That song essentially gets licensed by me for use, which means if it gets used or played in any commercial setting, I get paid.

Maximizing this same benefit (songwriting) is yet another

reason why Taylor Swift is such a great businesswoman on top of being a brilliant artist and one of the highest-grossing concert draws in country music. She writes all of her own songs, which means she owns the royalties, the publishing, the licensing, everything! Unlike many other singers who must sell concert tickets to get paid, she could stop touring today and still be among the highest paid artists in country music going forward!

The key is *how* you approach your investment decisions, whether investing your valuable time in creating instruments of passive income or whether investing the hard-earned money you've already made through some other means. The key principle I took away from Kiyosaki's *Rich Dad Poor Dad,* however, was the necessity of learning how to do it in the first place . . . anyway.

Money Rule #5: Insurance is not a luxury.

Plain and simple, proper insurance is an absolutely critical tool that can and likely will save you, your family, and/or your career one day. In fact it was the very experience of dealing with a house fire that taught me that I had never really had enough of it!

There are two categories of insurance that, even though they are not necessarily required by law, you must carry in order to protect yourself from being derailed: health insurance and liability insurance.

Health Insurance

I am utterly horrified by how many struggling artists I have met and continue to meet that will try to save a paltry $300 to $400 dollars a month by not purchasing any health insurance, while at the same time think nothing of eating out at restaurants or taking vacations that cost far more than that amount over the course of the same month!

By the age of thirty-five, I had already had two close friends who were diagnosed with multiple sclerosis, a disease that requires lifelong treatment. At least three friends of mine—younger than me—have been diagnosed with some form of cancer, and I can't even count how many friends of mine over the years have been waylaid by car accidents that, all too often, required multiple surgeries and medical bills that continued for years. Luckily all of my friends so far, except for one who had to declare bankruptcy, had health insurance when the unexpected happened.

Dr. David Himmelstein, associate professor of medicine at Harvard Medical School, was the lead author of a study that determined that medical bills are the leading cause of bankruptcy in the United States. In response to this finding, he was quoted as saying, "Unless you're Bill Gates, [without good insurance] you're just one serious illness away from bankruptcy. Most of the medically bankrupt were average Americans who happened to get sick." And that's just the health insurance side of it!

Liability Insurance

Any recognizable artist/celebrity has to contend with another unfortunate reality of living in the United States, and that is being singled out as a target for lawsuits. Even though it's far easier to become famous than rich these days, people who easily recognize you will assume you have money to spare and will often feel entitled to try to take it from you.

If you want to keep what you have (big or little), you need to actively protect it. Luckily there are several ways to do this, whether you create a Limited Liability Corporation (LLC) or whether you invest in any number of insurance options, such as

Learning how to protect your investments will require a bit of effort. But as I said already, becoming fully financially literate should be your second permanent job, and one that's just as important as your career itself.

maintaining high liability coverage on homes and vehicles or with an umbrella policy. I do all of these.

The recommended reading section of this book is chock full of the kinds of resources that can easily get you started. But don't stop there. You will likely find far more resources on your own that will uniquely tap your abilities to fund and protect all of your dreams much faster, and in ways that are far more interesting to you, but it's a good place to start!

At the beginning of your career, though, your first focus should be on protecting your greatest asset: you, which means you should make having health insurance an absolute priority, even if that means skipping a few other luxuries for a while.

As you progress, you will absolutely need to look into things like a self-employed workman's compensation policy in case you get hurt on the job (I cut the end of my left index finger off on *While You Were Out*), disability insurance in case you get hurt and aren't able to work for a period of time, and life insurance if *anyone* in your life depends on you financially.

A good financial advisor, or even just the Internet and a few good books, can help guide you through what types of insurance you need, how much you need, and when you need it. I can't imagine a situation much worse than having to forfeit your dreams to something unexpected yet so easily manageable just because you figured you could wait a little longer!

Insurance is the only fail-safe out there that is available to anyone who is capable of seeing its value enough to make it a priority ahead of time. Every single person I know who has ever been bitten by waiting to get insurance regrets it. I've seen people lose everything unnecessarily, including their lives, for simply thinking, "I'll get it eventually, I'm young." Or "I'm just trying to save right now." No excuses! Remember, as an entertainer, *you* are the product worth protecting at all costs!

Rule 10: Make the five money rules in this chapter your own in order to protect your career, and to become financially free regardless of how much money you make as an artist.

Using Emotional Alchemy to Get Work

Turning Fear and Other Negative Emotions into Power Tools

Of all the skills of the truly successful artists that I have touched on or will touch on, the ability to manage your emotions—to make them work for you instead of against you—is perhaps one of the most challenging things to fully embrace, and yet one of the most important skills you can ever acquire.

It's more than just the ability to keep a cool head in a crisis, although that's certainly the essence of it; but what gives a person an enormous leg up on others is the ability to take an emotion that paralyzes or diverts most people and actually use that negative emotion to their advantage. I call it emotional alchemy; turning emotional coal into gold. Examples of what I mean include:

- Being able to turn the fear and anxiousness that hit when heading into an audition into hyper-awareness and a supersharp mind by harnessing your natural adrenaline rush
- Turning frustration and the feeling of rejection into supercharged motivation

- Turning the feeling of being completely overwhelmed into a laser-sharp action plan for success that you didn't have before.

In this chapter, we will focus on the four most important emotions to alchemize for any artist—fear, frustration, feeling overwhelmed, and anger—along with several techniques for making the transformative leap from emotional coal to emotional gold.

The good news is that if any of the previously discussed six ways of thinking for success and any of the six traits of the successful artist have sunk in by now, then you are probably already turning much of your former roadblock emotions into power tools. Now we'll learn ways to sharpen them.

Fear

I'll start with fear, because it is by far the most paralyzing of all emotions for just about everyone. Studies have actually shown the fear of public speaking to be the number one human fear of working people. As far back as 1973, the *Times of London* reported that "41% of the 3000 respondents [surveyed] listed 'fear of public speaking' as their number one fear, while 19% listed 'death.'" Bigger than death—ouch!

Let's face it, every type of entertainment is merely a unique form of public speaking, be it dancing (communicating with our bodies), singing (communicating with our voices), playing a musical instrument (communicating through our instrument), acting (communicating with everything) . . . you get the point. So it stands to reason that entertainers, more than anyone else, will not only experience a higher level and frequency of fear than most working people on average, but artists therefore *must* learn to work through fear and with fear if they are to succeed.

Furthermore, as a performing artist, you—unofficially—sign a social contract ahead of time that allows and even encourages people to judge you publicly, and in often unnecessarily brutal ways. And that's just one thing to fear (if you choose). The list itself is as long as it is scary: fear of rejection, fear of humiliation, fear of forgetting your lines, fear of losing your place in the music, fear of freezing up, fear of the unknown, fear of fear, fear of mistakes, fear of failure, even fear of success! It goes on and on, and there's not enough space to cover all of them, and it would be pointless anyway.

Entertainers are a unique breed, not because we don't feel fear like everyone else but because we often seem to face a disproportionately greater amount of fear in order to succeed. It's one of the big reasons why we worship celebrities the way we do (even the not-so-talented ones) because they, at the very least, faced their fears in a way most "normal" people would find unimaginable.

It's a large reason why I find celebrity biographies so fascinating. I have always wanted to find out what fears they faced and how they handled them in a desperate attempt to learn how to better face my own. I figured they all had to have found a way to handle it, and what I found were much of the same techniques used by pretty much everyone. The most successful people were even able to *use* fear to their advantage, much the way a Jujitsu master uses an attacker's energy against him, rather than directly opposing it.

On the other end of the spectrum, going head to head with fear on fear's terms is where paralysis comes from and is a great way to end your career before it ever begins. Pure and simple, the power of fear, when harnessed, can give us distinct and profound advantages in our career.

I have often found that I've even craved fear in a given situation, having seen how it has helped me do things in the past that I thought were impossible, like sing a high G eight shows a week when I'm normally only capable of an F in rehearsal.

What Is Fear?

First we must understand exactly what purpose fear has served us as human beings so that we can decide how to better use it.

At the core, fear is really two things: a physical response and a survival tool.

Fear is a physical response—in other words, we feel it. This is a critical thing to understand, since the best way to deal with any physical challenge is with physical conditioning. Think for a second how you feel after a good workout: as if you can handle anything, right? Condition the body, and you are also conditioning the mind to handle more stress, the same physical stress we feel when we are scared. So the first tool you have to combat fear at the source is through physical exercise. This could be as simple as making sure to take a brisk walk just before tackling a scary situation in order to get your endorphins going to your advantage.

But aside from the physical response, the primary purpose of fear in human history has been for survival. Therefore, it can't be all bad, right? Fear warns us of danger, gives us an adrenaline rush needed for our fight-or-flight response, heightens all five of our senses, and reminds us to get prepared.

Fear can trip us up, though: survival is not the same thing as thriving. Survival is defensive and thriving is progressive. Once again, we can thank our societal training for teaching us to be terrified of things that won't harm us physically. For example, we are taught—and constantly reminded—in school, by our parents, friends, family, the workplace, on TV, radio, everywhere, that we are constantly being judged and that to fall short in someone else's estimation means humiliation and ridicule.

So anytime we are in a situation in which we'll be judged, we get scared. All of a sudden we get a surge of adrenaline, often manifested as panic, and we try like hell to simply avoid the scenario altogether as if it were a hungry lion. That's our flight response.

Repetition of the same scenario over and over again has reassured us that fleeing this situation can almost always allow us to avoid judgment, which will almost always avoid any chance of humiliation and ridicule. It also guarantees that you'll never go anywhere or do anything new or interesting because of another fact of life: without risk there's no reward.

The Art of Mental Jujitsu

As entertainers, we're after the reward, so we need to train ourselves to harness the power of fear to trigger the *fight* response instead, because after all, to be an entertainer literally means to place yourself in the line of humiliation and ridicule fire. To do that, you will have to fight your fear using mental jujitsu.

If you're saying, *Well, I'm not a fighter,* I can tell you this: everyone was a fighter at birth. No one fights harder to survive than a newborn, and they do it instinctively. Fighting as an adult, however, is something you learn.

Several biographies of Muhammad Ali point to his personal experience of fear—having grown up in the racially charged culture of 1940s Louisville, Kentucky—as being a major driving force in his becoming the most celebrated World Heavyweight Champion in the history of boxing. What Muhammad Ali learned, among other key principles, is that the first rule to dealing with fear is to listen to what the emotion is saying, and that is: "Get prepared!" I've already mentioned the critical physical training component, but this is also where the artistic training, research, education, and experience come in.

From the moment you decided to become a professional artist, there were never going to be any shortcuts, no matter what we have been sold about the existence of an overnight success, being discovered, or winning a competition and then bam, easy sailing. These, I hope you know by now, are just myths.

Simply put, the more you prepare, the less you feel fear.

Almost everyone has had the recurring nightmare in which we show up to class only to find out that there was an exam that day that we didn't prepare for. Most of us have also had the real-life experience of showing up for actual exams that we were well prepared for and being barely nervous at all.

But Don't Overdo It

There is a limit to preparation, however, and at some point we have to face unknown variables blindly. We have to be wary of the trap of falling in love with the security that perpetual training provides and not ever letting go and taking the risk regardless of how ready you feel. I have friends who have five academic degrees because they became addicted to the security of higher education and couldn't make the leap into the real world!

So how do you know when you're ready to take the leap? While it's easy to just say "instinct," the reality is that you'll never know for sure. Also remember that a teacher who depends on you for income may never be inclined to tell you that they think you're ready—after all, the minute they push you out of the nest, you stop paying them!

The rule of thumb I've used with great success is this:

The second I find myself wondering if I'm ready, I take the risk.

I've come to realize that the "wonder" is my instinct speaking to me! It doesn't matter whether it's an audition, an interview, mixing a demo CD, whatever . . . when I hear myself asking this question, I don't hesitate, I don't think twice, I don't analyze: it's go time. (Note: this excludes extreme sports like skydiving—I wait till I'm fairly certain on those.)

I made that simple agreement with myself at the start of my career, and I follow it religiously. It's paid off more often than not, and the few times I found that I could have been more prepared served only to show me exactly what I needed to work on and, more importantly, served to help me more finely tune my barometer of "ready-ness" so that I could make the assessment far more quickly and accurately in the future.

It's a win-win rule, and I suggest you start practicing it in your everyday decisions so that when the big emotional risks pop up, you'll be ready!

So You're Ready . . .

You've taken the anticipation/fear either out of the equation or at least down to a manageable, "I'm-ready-for-the-exam" level of nervousness through physical and mental preparation. All that's left to face now is the in-the-moment fear that you'll be required to overcome, and it just so happens that this aspect of fear is the most difficult one to control. This is where the following tools will take you through the door. Once you have a few successes under your belt, you'll find that you will very quickly ratchet up your tolerance for fear!

Four Ways to Use Fear to Your Advantage

1. Ask Three Magic Questions

- What's the worst that can happen? (Would it be a life/career ender? Would the damage be permanent?)
- How could you repair the damage if necessary? (How long would this take?)
- What would you lose if you didn't take this risk? (The opportunity of a lifetime and all that entails, for example?)

Yep, most of our fears are completely irrational. For example, it's a simple fact that flying in a commercial jet is far safer than driving in a car, even in this terrorism-charged post-9/11 world. Yet flying holds a special place for fear in many psyches.

In fact, a statistical analysis conducted by German psychologist Gerd Gigerenzer (cited in the book *The Science of Fear* by Daniel Gardner) showed that the decrease in air travel the year after the 9/11 attacks correlated directly to 1,595 more people dying in car accidents that same year as the population suddenly began to avoid flying. That's over half the number of people who died in the attacks on September 11th and six times the number of people who were actually on board those doomed planes themselves.

Since most fears are irrational anyway, it's pretty helpful to first define exactly what it is we're scared of and then consider the worst-case scenario. It's an eye-opening process and it almost immediately clears the fog of the fear emotions. When it comes to facing a terrifying challenge, just asking yourself the three questions above provides a true assessment of what's really at stake . . . or more aptly what's *not* really at stake! I guarantee that by the end of this process you'll feel quite a bit better, because the conditioned emotions are eliminated from the equation and you can deal with facts. This will, in essence, shore up your emotional anti-fear foundation at the base level.

2. Surrender

As I've already mentioned, it's counterproductive to fight fear on fear's terms. It's far too powerful; confronting it directly often just seems to amplify its power. We end up wallowing in negative scenarios that build on each other until eventually we become paralyzed. Like a Jujitsu master, you must first accept the fear, welcome it, and then redirect it to your advantage. The hardest step, though, is just saying to yourself, "I'm scared to death, and that's OK."

The next step is to remind yourself why it's not only OK to be scared (because it means you're human) but it's also a good thing, because it gives you tools that can be used to your advantage. Those tools come in the form of heightened senses thanks to adrenaline, the gift of human survival. Once we stop fighting the adrenalized senses by first surrendering, we can then redirect them to our advantage.

3. Redirect

Adrenaline is nature's most powerful drug, and we cannot underestimate how it heightens and sharpens all of our senses. In survival situations, it has given people superhuman strength, enabling them to lift a car off a loved one or increased reaction speed, slowing down perception of time, with people even reporting the ability to literally see a bullet whiz past them!

For public speaking, auditions, performances, and important meetings, we also have the same heightened senses that can be relied on for peak performance. Just like the survival situations, your reaction time will speed up and you will sometimes, in the moment, feel smarter, more agile, and on top of your game. It's what people often refer to as being "in the zone," where the right words, thoughts, jokes, etc. just pop into your head at the right time.

Physically, you'll also have the increased physical strength and agility, which, if you embrace it, very often gets translated to observers as *confidence,* as your natural posture will be one of power (ostensibly to scare away predators). Have you ever heard someone say to you, "You sure didn't seem nervous"? Simply being aware that your fear is actually sending a message of confidence is an enormous tool in and of itself.

With all of your senses heightened, you'll be able to quickly assess things better, read people better, and react to unforeseen challenges without thinking.

I've often gone into auditions literally counting on these aspects to come through, knowing I wasn't as prepared as I could have been. While this is not a recommended substitute for preparation, I did book my first role in a movie, *Shaft Returns,* with a cold read. I wasn't given the audition "sides" (audition pages from the script) beforehand, and when I arrived at the casting agency I was rushed into the room without any chance to preview the lines whatsoever. Reading right off the page with my adrenaline pumping I nailed it and beat out several hundred or more other actors for the part. Even though most of my scenes got left on the cutting room floor in the final film, I had the experience of working with Christian Bale, Samuel Jackson, Toni Collette, and John Singleton as my introduction to film acting!

That on-the-job training, by the way was, in my opinion, worth a *thousand* film acting classes and instead of paying for it, I got paid ten thousand a week for three straight weeks . . . and I still get residuals checks today!

4. Go Five Feet: The Art of the Baby Step

The final frontier of managing your fear once you've prepared for the situation as much as is reasonable, and now that you've acknowledged fear, redirecting to your advantage adrenaline's power to heighten your senses, is taking a leap of faith.

Even at this stage, having done all of the prep work, this prospect may still seem overwhelming. That's perfectly normal. Anyone who goes into an audition or important meeting of some sort without major butterflies is either lying about it, crazy, or both. But the ability to "Just do it . . . *anyway*" is what separates the successes from the painfully boring existences.

The only tool I know of (still searching!) for adding the "anyway" to the end of Nike's "Just Do It" in this scenario is to break up your challenge into tiny pieces and only focus on one tiny piece at a time.

I call it going five more feet, which is the agreement I made with myself years ago at mile twenty of the New York City marathon. I had hit the wall, was scared to keep moving, scared to stop, scared to fail, and my brain kept telling me that I was heading for a month of traction in the hospital . . . but for the last 6.2 miles I only ran five feet at a time.

The same applies when you're dealing with the classic stage fright. Simply make an agreement with yourself to show up to the building; then make an agreement with yourself to go in the door; then onto the stage; then to open your mouth; and so on. The key to this working, though, is to not even think about going through the door, going on stage, or opening your mouth until you first show up to the building!

With each step, you can give yourself full permission to bail out at any point. I have found, as my mother taught me, that just allowing yourself the "out option" is often enough to never have to use it. In actual practice, bailing out rarely happens because at each step of the way you find it really wasn't that bad and, more importantly, you develop momentum. By then you're experiencing the positives of both adrenaline and a few mini-successes already, and that usually feels better and better as you go, until you're "in the zone."

I'll never forget a moment in my career when this all came together at a pivotal point and a nearly paralyzing fear could have significantly delayed, or even prevented, my career from really taking off. I had literally just landed at JFK from my whirlwind tour with Ha-Ha (pronounced "na-na"), a Russian rock band, when I got a page (remember beepers?) from my agent saying he had an audition for me that afternoon to be the cohost of the hit TV series *America's Funniest Home Videos,* along with Daisy Fuentes.

To make it to the audition on time, I would have to go straight to the ABC offices from the airport. What terrified me was the fact that they were only seeing stand-up comics, which my agent assured them I was (though I wasn't), and that part of the audition required us to perform a ten-minute comedic monologue on camera, which my agent had assured them I could do (I had prepared nothing of the sort).

Considering the fact that I had never done stand-up comedy, and considering the fact that I didn't have any time to even steal a ten-minute monologue, much less write one, I was scared to death. To make things worse, the audition was being run by one of the top casting directors at ABC, and my agent made sure to remind me how critical this meeting was, as she doesn't see *just anyone.* Great!

Just as the whole notion of what I was facing started to over-whelm me, I decided to simply focus on retrieving my baggage. Then I decided I'd hop a cab in the general direction of the audition, and I told myself I could always use the excuse of just having flown in from Russia, traffic, etc., if I decided to bail, but I'd at least go that far.

In the cab I freaked out a bit, but I figured that at the bare minimum I would see if I could come up with anything funny to say about Bob Sagat, the soon-to-be-replaced host of *Amer-*

ica's Funniest Home Videos (that turned out to be easier than I thought), and Daisy Fuentes, the already hired female cohost.

Once again, I told myself that if I wasn't able to come up with anything suitable, I would give myself full permission to bail out.

Then the cab arrived at ABC, so I decided I'd at least go up and say hello, thinking I could always lean on my two huge suitcases as an excuse if I really sucked; after all, most of the other stand-up comics auditioning probably didn't just get off a plane from a stadium tour in Russia. It was, I figured, a fairly good (at the very least true) story, and hopefully the casting director, I reasoned, would at least think that was impressive.

With each little step, I only had to so much as go another metaphorical five feet. This process of taking baby steps entirely eliminated the overwhelming, "What the hell am I gonna do?" aspect of the challenge I faced, and before I knew it, I was standing at the casting room door, committed to going into the room where the casting director stood with her video camera.

All she said to me was, "OK, slate (which is industry-speak for state your name and representing agency) and then do your stand up bit, and . . . *go!*" The record light went on the camera and bam . . . the adrenaline rush kicked in . . . and I was on. My loosely formed jokes about Bob Sagat's comedy being used in Texas prisons for punishment and the idea that I was actually there as Daisy Fuentes's stalker materialized on the spot in a fluid stream of consciousness. I even found myself improvising new jokes. About five minutes into this somewhat out-of-body experience, I was on such a high that I felt like I could have gone an hour.

At about ten minutes in, the casting director, who had been shaking her head with incredulous laughter throughout, stopped the camera and abruptly said, "Well, that will get you a flight out to LA." She thanked me and only then asked about my two huge suitcases, which now seemed to be an even cooler segue into my Russia story than using them as an excuse for a poor performance would have ever been.

At any rate, I had earned my first screen test of my career, and that year I ended up screen testing for three other shows, including an hour-long drama for CBS that was never made and two sitcoms for Warner Brothers.

The critical element that got me through this horrific challenge of pretending to be a standup even though I couldn't have been less prepared for it was that I never committed to the whole process all at once. That would have been way too overwhelming. Instead, I only went five feet, and then another, and another, until it was all said and done.

Postscript: Even though I didn't get that job, or even the next three I tested for, I was now being taken seriously as a contender for real A-list jobs on television, and in the world of entertainment, that's one of your biggest victories—being welcomed to the game. As a result, my ability to perform under extreme pressure also had a huge impact on not just how my agent saw me from then on, but more importantly on how I saw *myself*. And it wasn't long after that that I was officially playing ball. But I had to face the fear first, five feet at a time!

Frustration

Frustration comes in many forms: disappointment, rejection, feeling inadequate, impatience, etc., but however it shows up, a successful artist must learn to transform that frustration into victories rather than giving up or backing off.

It was frustration that nearly made both James Van Der Beek and Robert Pattinson decide to quit the business entirely, just one day before they went on *one last audition* and booked their career-making role.

It was the ability to manage his frustration that kept Harrison Ford in Los Angeles plugging away year after year, for ten whole years, before his big break.

The message that frustration sends is actually a positive one, because feeling frustrated means you have higher expectations for yourself than the results you're getting. That's good, because higher expectations take us to higher places. High expectations are also born out of competence and having been successful before! Now all you need to do is to figure out why you haven't gotten there yet and adjust your sails accordingly!

The trick to turning frustration into a power tool is, once again, asking the right questions. Here are six questions you should ask yourself to help turn frustration into gold:

1. What did this result teach me?
2. What new information could I research to help me?
3. How can I go about this differently?
4. How did [insert your idol here] handle this same challenge?
5. Are my current expectations realistic at this moment, or do I need to break up my goal into smaller steps?
6. What new skills do I need to acquire?

When the frustration turns from being something that makes you want to bang your head against a wall (or worse, quit) into answers to these six questions, you're no longer living with the self-defeating emotion you started with. You're already transformed! Your focus cannot possibly remain in the frustration now that it has a bunch of exciting answers and opportunities to explore that are impossible to ignore!

Feeling Overwhelmed

Like the emotion of frustration, feeling overwhelmed also comes in many forms, whether it's panic, a sense of hopelessness, or even the omnipresent condition of depression that we hear about so much. I did an online search for "famous people with depression," and the list that came up was nothing short of heartbreaking.

There are certainly forms of depression that I believe must

be treated by a qualified doctor and should be taken seriously. There are also many less serious forms that can be treated with behavior modification, as was illustrated in the UC Berkeley study I cited in chapter 8, in which people with clinically diagnosed depression were cured, at least temporarily, simply by smiling into a mirror for twenty-minute sessions for four weeks.

True clinical neurological diagnosis and therapies aside, there are a few practical techniques I have found that greatly reduce, if not eliminate, the more common feeling of being overwhelmed, and the first thing that you likely need to do is to re-prioritize.

I'm a doer by nature. I love challenges, I love pleasing people, and I love problem-solving. The problem is that in reality you just can't take on every challenge, please everyone, and solve every problem. Sometimes my unconscious mind decides that I can anyway, and in those cases, I always end up overwhelmed, panicked, and at times even depressed, thinking that any action on my part is hopeless. I'm sure I don't have to tell you how counterproductive these feelings are, as they all lead to one single result: shutting down.

What I've realized is that nearly every time I've felt this way, I had been giving equal priority to things that were never of equal importance. The key is to step back and reassess what's really most important, not only in accomplishing your goals, but to your values, and then concentrate only on the first things first until you're back on track. This means putting everything else aside, including the second-most-important thing on your list, until that very first thing on your list is addressed fully.

This creates a revised action plan, a turn-by-turn road map, to the destination that's really truly important to you, including your career in entertainment.

By far the best example of this concept I've ever seen comes from Steven Covey's 1994 best-selling book *First Things First,* a book I read while studying the secrets of Fortune 500 companies in college:

I attended a seminar once where the instructor was lecturing on time. At one point, he said, "Okay, it's time for a quiz." He reached under the table and pulled out a wide-mouthed gallon jar. He set it on the table next to a platter covered with fist-sized rocks on it. "How many of these rocks do you think we can get in the jar?" he asked.

After we made our guess, he said, "Okay. Let's find out." He set one rock in the jar . . . then another . . . then another. I don't remember how many he got in, but he got the jar full. Then he asked, "Is that jar full?"

Everybody looked at the rocks and said, "Yes."

Then he said, "Ahhh." He reached under the table and pulled out a bucket of gravel. Then he dumped some gravel in and shook the jar and the gravel went in all the little spaces left by the big rocks. Then he grinned and said once more, "Is the jar full?"

By this time we were onto him. "Probably not," we said.

"Good!" he replied. And he reached under the table and brought out a bucket of sand. He started dumping the sand in and it went in all the little spaces left by the rocks and the gravel. Once more he looked at us and said, "Is the jar full?"

"No!" we all roared.

He said, "Good!" and he grabbed a pitcher of water and began to pour it in. He got something like a quart of water in that jar. Then he said, "Well, what's the point?"

Somebody said, "Well, there are gaps, and if you really work at it, you can always fit more into your life."

"No," he said, "That's not the point. The point is: if you hadn't put these big rocks in first, would you ever have gotten any of them in?"

The same is true with life. If we don't identify the big rocks—the most important things in our lives—and if we don't make them our absolute priority, we end up with a life (jar) full of all the unimportant stuff, with no more room for the big/important stuff anymore. Any time you find yourself run ragged and are neglecting what's truly important to you, it will always lead to being overwhelmed!

This can and will likely happen at every stage in your entertainment career, whether you're just starting out and are running around town meeting other actors, musicians, fellow waiters, or checking in with social media for five hours straight, when you probably should be home editing a reel to email to agents or perfecting that piano concerto or monologue for an audition, or whether you wake up one day managing all the people you've hired along the way to manage your crazy life: managers, business managers, your publicist, the housekeeper. Regardless of how successful you are or how you got there, the solution always begins with emptying that jar and putting the big rocks back in first.

The Myth of Multitasking

An enormous cause of stress, anxiety, and the feeling of being overwhelmed can come from an age-old phenomenon that has been greatly exacerbated by our entrance into the information age, and that is the idea that multitasking is a good thing. In actual practice, it is not only a major contributor to that overwhelmed feeling, but it is actually extremely inefficient, despite what most people think.

A book that I believe everyone should be forced to read before they ever receive their first cell phone or, God forbid, a driver's license, is *The Myth of Multitasking,* by Dave Crenshaw. It's a tiny book, but it completely debunks the myth that we—and I include myself in this—have all bought into at some point in our lives.

In the book, Crenshaw cites several studies that demonstrate that human beings, at best, only have the ability to *background-task,* described as "when you perform two or more tasks where only one of those tasks requires mental effort . . . like eating dinner and watching TV, or jogging and listening to music." What most people typically think of as multitasking is, in actuality, just *switchtasking,* or switching attention back and forth from one task to another.

René Marois, Ph.D., from the department of psychology at Vanderbilt University, states, "Our new research offers neurological evidence that the brain cannot effectively do two things at once." As a result, each time you change focus, you lose a significant amount of time, simply because you have to reacquaint yourself with each situation, not to mention the fact that the quality of your attention is significantly diminished by the stress of disorientation. The result? A constant sense of disorientation, stress, and feeling of being overwhelmed.

To illustrate the inefficiency of switchtasking, Crenshaw instructs a subject to write a sentence one letter at a time. After writing each letter, the person must write a 1, then 2, then 3, and so on, below each letter, while being timed. Crenshaw then has the same person do the first task fully before the second, in other words, write the complete sentence first and then the complete list of corresponding numbers below it; this test is also timed.

On average, a person is twice as fast when focused on the single task of writing a sentence first and then numbering as when switchtasking. Also, most people tend to make a few errors in the first exercise (when they were switchtasking), and they rarely make any in the second (when they weren't)! The moral is scary: by switchtasking, we actually take twice as long to do something, and we make more mistakes!

So if you're someone who prides himself or herself on being a great multitasker, by now I hope you realize that you've really only been a frequent switchtasker who's probably overwhelmed most of the time, who makes unnecessary mistakes, and who is only half as efficient with your time as you could be! That's great news, because it's an easy fix!

And let me dispel one last possibly common assumption: in the August 2005 issue of the *Journal of Experimental Psychology,* professor of psychology David E. Meyer states, "In our particular study, where we brought both young males and young females—college students—into the lab, there was no evidence whatsoever of any gender difference in [switchtasking] performance."

Just think what you could do with twice the hours, half the mistakes, and a relaxed state of mind!

Here are seven of Crenshaw's tips that I've adapted for getting there:

1. Recognize that multitasking is a myth.
2. Schedule one specific time daily with the people who tend to interrupt you most throughout the day in order to give them your full attention.
3. Set expectations and create personal "shop hours" to let people know when you will be available.
4. Resist making *active switches* (times when you decide to interrupt yourself by checking email, checking in with friends, social media, etc.), especially while driving!
5. Minimize *passive switches* (turn off automatic email alerts, text alerts, turn your cell phone ringer off during focus time, etc.) To help with this, create an outgoing voicemail message and auto-email/text replies that state that you check them at specific times (i.e., 10 a.m. and 2 p.m.) and that you will return the call/email/request at that time.
6. With your time prioritized and potential distractions scheduled, give every task and every person your full attention when dealing with them, before moving on to something else.
7. Never commit to something without your calendar in hand.

Anger

One day while I was living and auditioning as an actor in LA, a friend of mine came by to tell me what had just happened to him at a general audition, which is a meeting in which casting directors will see new people even if they don't have a specific job in mind. They do this simply to keep up with the talent pool. My friend's agent had managed to set him up with one of the biggest casting directors in LA at the time.

This was, needless to say, a fairly big deal and a great opportunity for him to make a first and lasting impression on the type of person who has the power to make a career. My friend, incidentally, just so happens to be one of the most talented actors I have ever seen, but unfortunately, he's also a hothead.

So, as the story goes, he walked into the casting director's office full of excitement and was asked to sit down across the desk while the casting director finished a phone call. Five minutes later, the call was over and the meeting began, but my friend wasn't able to so much as say hello before another call came in, and the casting director took the call. This apparently happened a few more times, and in addition, an assistant pulled the casting director out of the office for a few minutes to handle some kind of "casting emergency."

By the fourth phone call and about thirty minutes later, my friend was fuming. This time, the casting director appeared to be on a personal call that also seemed not to be ending any time soon. Nearing explosion, my friend picked up some packing tape that he noticed lying on the casting director's desk and began wrapping the tape around his own head and body and then around the chair he was sitting in. By the time he was done—and miraculously without managing to draw any notice from the casting director, who was looking out the window, completely engrossed in his phone conversation—he had successfully taped himself to the chair so completely that he had to be cut out of it.

The phone call ended and my friend was promptly cut free and excused very unceremoniously. He lost his agent and never worked a day in an industry that I firmly believe he could easily have taken by storm . . . if not for his inability to manage his anger.

When I asked him what he was thinking, he said he wasn't, and that taping himself to the chair was the only act he could think of that kept him from leaping across the desk and punching the guy! I couldn't believe it!

The truly sad part of the story is that this situation was actually an amazing opportunity for my friend to turn his anger into career gold. To do that, however, he would've had to understand what his anger was telling him. In most cases, it's usually the same thing: that you feel violated in some way. This either means that you haven't communicated your personal values to someone clearly—in this case, that you believe it's important to respect other people's time—or that you are actually misinterpreting the situation.

What if my friend incorrectly assumed that the casting director's personal call wasn't important? Perhaps it was, in fact, his attempt to console and uplift the spirits of his dying mother when he realized, in that very moment, that he wouldn't be able to be bedside with her as she passed away! It's an extreme example, sure, but this could have also explained the casting director's distracted state of mind under that kind of stress!

The bottom line is this: regardless, my friend could have and should have done things very differently in that situation in order to communicate his values while not jumping to conclusions.

Always Allow People to Save Face

There are many ways my friend could have turned that situation around to his favor. Here's just one: after thirty minutes of suffering such an indignity, my friend could have taken a moment to write a simple note that said something like: "So sorry, I have another appointment I need to run to. I would really love to reschedule when it's better for you if possible," signing it with his name, agent's name, and phone number.

He could've dropped the note on the casting director's

desk, smiled, and walked out. This would have communicated to the casting director that he was worthy of his undivided attention, someone who's in demand with other appointments, while also gently sending the message that he has self-respect (an under-celebrated asset in Hollywood). Most importantly, though, by choosing this action he would have also allowed the casting director to save face. In essence this "gift" of saving face acts as a kind of "You owe me one!" marker that can be very effective.

Instead of ruining his own future career, as he likely did with his childish maneuver, my friend would have undoubtedly guaranteed a second opportunity to showcase his talents for an extremely powerful man, who would almost certainly give him 100 percent of his attention the next time. Furthermore, this powerful man would more or less know that he owed my friend a favor! That's alchemy!

The solution to turning a situation that makes you angry into a golden opportunity starts with recognizing that most gut reactions to anger almost never help your cause, as was demonstrated with my friend's reaction. Once we calm ourselves enough to accept this, we can then move on to real alchemy by asking ourselves the following questions:

- What is, bottom line, the best-case scenario result I could get here? For my friend this would have been a second meeting with a man who's powerful and who owes him one.

- Could I possibly be misinterpreting this scenario? In my friend's case, it's hard to argue that the casting director wasn't being rude, but all too frequently we just need to change our perspective to see that we're merely overreacting or that we simply haven't made our own values or personal standards very clear in the first place. This leads to the third question.

- Have I clearly communicated my values or standards to this person? By politely excusing himself for another "appointment" with a note, my friend could have set the stage for respect the next time without ruffling feathers unnecessarily. Which brings us to the follow-up to the first question.

- How can I achieve my best-case scenario result? Once you've sorted out, in a clear-headed way, whether or not you are indeed correctly interpreting the scenario that angered you and whether or not the person did in fact violate your clearly defined standards (or, more likely, that your values or standards simply were not communicated well), then you're in a position to figure out how to get your ideal bottom line, while allowing that person the gift of saving face.

Pavlov's Dogs

This anger-alchemy process does, however, require a moment of pausing and stepping back in the heat of the moment—a very difficult thing to do. But with a little conditioned reflex practice, it can alter your entire life and perhaps save your career!

The man credited with pioneering the concept of *conditioned reflex* is Russian physiologist Ivan Pavlov. He developed his theory while studying the digestive system of dogs. For his experiments, he needed a reliable way to get the dogs to salivate every time he needed to conduct his digestive tests. He discovered that by ringing a bell each time the dog was fed, he could condition the dog to salivate at the sound of the bell, and he no longer even needed to actually feed the dog each time, just ring the bell.

Inserting a pause before reacting with a hothead requires the same sort of conditioning. Most of us are already hyper-aware of that first moment when our blood gets boiling, so the first thing to do is to acknowledge this moment verbally to yourself, even if it's just in your head: "Yep, I'm mad now!"

For me, I hear a bell in my head each time someone crosses the line, then—like something out of a cartoon—"ding," a bubble goes over my head that says, "I'm mad!" Hearing that bell (or just recognizing it) allows you to attach the pause. Mad—bell—pause. Mad—bell—pause.

Once the pause becomes automatic, the most critical question to ask in that pause is "What do I want my best-case scenario outcome to be?" Often just asking the question is enough to diffuse a potentially disastrous situation and prevent a regrettable response.

With a little practice, you'll be able to go beyond merely "diffusing" your own anger to turning the situation into pure opportunity by answering the rest of the questions.

> **Rule 11: Begin to use the emotions of fear, frustration, feeling overwhelmed, and anger to your advantage by using the techniques described, as well as by seeking out other available techniques.**

Networking: Be a Dog

YOU WILL NOT get very far in entertainment without mastering the skill of networking. Everyone knows that networking exponentially increases your possible opportunities through expanding your connections; but what too many people fail to realize is that your ability to network effectively also serves to showcase your ability to sell your product: you.

At some point down the road, someone who hires you will expect you to help sell the project you're a part of to the public, whether at a press junket, an industry event, or another type of presentation. So it stands to reason that if, while networking, you impress a potential employer with your networking skill (which is basically selling), they'll likely see you as an exceptional asset and will more likely want to hire you!

Why Artists Need to Be Dogs

An embarrassing reality of human nature is that we are all self-obsessed to some degree, like it or not. Dale Carnegie, in *How to Win Friends and Influence People,* wrote:

The New York telephone company made a detailed

study of telephone conversations to find out which word is the most frequently used [and] it is the personal pronoun "I." "I." "I." It was used 3,900 times in 500 telephone conversations. "I." "I." "I." "I."

When you see a group photograph that you are in, whose picture do you look for first?

Carnegie goes on to offer perhaps the single most valuable piece of advice ever written when it comes to networking: "You can make more friends in two months by becoming interested in other people than you can in two years by trying to get other people interested in you."

And yet, as entertainers, we tend to be the most egregious violators of this principle—the very nature of our business cries, "Hey, look at me!" Enter, stage right, one of the biggest reasons most talented entertainers never find success: poor or, even worse, non-existent networking skills.

Carnegie goes on to suggest, "Why not study the technique of the greatest winner of friends the world has ever known?" *Dogs!* Dogs are only interested in you, never themselves, they greet total strangers with adoring affection, and they always go out of their way just to meet you. They want to know everything about you (the welcome sniff), they're always glad to see you, there's never an ulterior motive, they're loyal, and they're grateful for *any* amount of time you have for them, no matter how big or small.

To effectively network, you must have a basic understanding of people's needs and learn the basic art of endearing yourself to them sincerely. In other words, you need to learn how to be less self-absorbed all the time.

For our purposes, let's define *networking* as "the process of actively building a collection of friends and associates who are potentially in a position to help you achieve your goals and would like to see you succeed at achieving your goals."

The Six Basic Rules of Networking—From a Dog's Perspective

1. *What would Wolfie do?* Networking is not a tool. It is a way of life. It's not about "getting" something you want, but rather it's about creating an environment of relationships in which people want to help you because you sincerely care for and help them without any expectations.

This principle speaks, once again, to the ideal of integrity and defines why dogs are man's best friend: the main reason? Dogs give love unconditionally!

If you approach networking from an entirely selfish point of view, it will be obvious to others . . . at least eventually. In other words, don't ever pretend to be interested in someone or their interests. If you can't find something in common to sincerely care about, then just focus on being professional, good at your craft, and likable in a general sense. Remember: you can't be all things to all people, but you can always be sincere!

2. *Jump the fence.* To build a network you must go to the people you wish to be around.

It's highly unlikely that, while you're just sitting in the corner of a cafe being brilliant, the people you dream of being around will come to you. Just like the friendly dog, you have to occasionally jump the fence in order to meet people, and you have to learn to introduce yourself to strangers.

3. *Run in packs.* The bigger and more diverse the network, the greater potential for opportunities. But . . .

4. *Always be loyal to the one that puts food in your bowl.* In other words: don't overextend yourself!

Although a bigger network provides more opportunities in one sense, remember to only ever take on that which you can realistically nurture with your sincere attention. Overextending yourself will always work against you in the long run, since it's impossible to be sincerely interested in and attentive to everyone.

People who feel they are being used will often put just as much effort into thwarting your goals than a friend would into helping you achieve them. You may wake up one day to an empty bowl! Which is why . . .

5. *Dogs sniff butts, not _ssholes.* Choose your friends and associates carefully.

As I've suggested before, you simply can't afford to spend all of your time taking in every wounded bird you meet, and you may have to cut ties with people who are also fulltime "takers": people who aren't mutually interested in your well-being. Just as your intentions for being kind and generous to others must be sincere and without expectations, so should the people you network with be, whether they are part of your specific career network or friends.

6. *Even a dog knows its name!* "Remember that a person's name is to that person the sweetest and most important sound in any language." (Dale Carnegie)

It's amazing to me that the phrase "I'm terrible with names," is so frequently uttered today that it seems almost forgivable. To be "bad" with names is to loudly announce to everyone that you are so self-absorbed that you simply don't have the time to bother learning the one word (*one* little word) that happens to uniquely identify every person in the world as an individual. Names are so important to most people that many will even give millions of dollars to have theirs attached to a building, stadium, or library so that it will stick around long after they're gone.

If you do nothing else today, do yourself a huge favor and make learning how to remember names of people you meet your absolute number-one priority!

Memory experts have discovered that the human memory

has an extremely strong visual component. The problem for most people is that names are abstract. This makes names more difficult to remember than things that you can easily picture in your head. (You can't picture a "Jen" as easily as a "hen.")

Luckily there are a million and one tricks to make this a relatively easy and even fun skill to acquire. Most importantly, it will give you a huge advantage over those who never come to realize the power of remembering names. I use four different techniques to remember names and faces:

1. I always make sure I hear the name clearly, and I always ask them to repeat it if I'm not 100 percent sure I did. Even this act tells the person you've just met that you care enough about them to get their name right!

2. I always make sure I use their name immediately and often from the get-go. "Well, Garrison, it's really great to finally meet you," or "Hey, Garrison, let me ask you something. . . ." Another great way to do this is to immediately introduce the person you just met, by name, to another person.

3. I also try to immediately make a very wacky visual and verbal connection between their name and some aspect of their physicality so that I can put a face to their name later on. For example: Say Jen has a long neck, I may (in my head only!) say "Jen the long-necked Hen" and then picture a hen with a giraffe's neck. The more ludicrous the association the better, as it triggers the creative part of the brain that's linked to memory.

4. The last thing I always try to do is to get a business card so that I can see their name in writing, which also triggers the memory nerves. If I'm in a crowded setting, I may also try to occasionally step away from the fray to write down names and descriptions of people I have met if possible.

These techniques have served me well over the years, and I have yet to find ones that work better or more consistently for me. Because everyone operates differently, however, I highly recommend researching other techniques as well. You can find countless memory-improving techniques on the Internet and in books.

The most comprehensive book I know of that teaches easy-to-learn memory systems (including some of the techniques I've mentioned already) is by memory experts Harry Lorayne and Jerry Lucas and has the easy-to-remember title *The Memory Book.* Lorayne and Lucas are the kind of guys you may have seen performing memory feats on late-night shows as they memorize, in a few minutes, two hundred audience members' names and where they're from and then recite them flawlessly. Incidentally, this book (or others like it) will also help any actor, musician, dancer, or anyone whose job will require them to quickly learn scripts, lyrics, dance sequences, etc.

A Final Word on Names

I've often found that it's just as important to be *noticed* remembering people's names by others as it is to actually remember a single person's name in the first place. I'll never forget being told once by the director of a TV show I was working on how impressed he was that I called every crew member on set (and there were many) by their first name, no matter how big or small their title. That director has been the source of many other jobs for me, and I can't help but think that this one thing that impressed him so much was a main reason.

Begin Quality Networking Today

In the technological world of today, especially with the invention of social media, there are so many ways to network that it has actually effectively diluted the value of a network, essentially replacing the *quality* of relationships with *quantity.* This is bad, since any network is almost worthless without a truly sincere connection.

It's easy to build up online networking sites and instant

blogs with thousands and even millions of "friends," "follow-ers," or "network-ees" and yet still have no true connections to the people you're supposedly connected to! While these outlets can and should be a part of your "networking arsenal," they can also be a great time suck, which could ultimately derail you from far more important and effective efforts while providing you very little actual return.

One thing has not changed, according to most sociologists, when it comes to networking, regardless of the advances in technology, and that is: the highest quality forms of communi-cation have always been directly related to the quantity of inter-action with the five senses. When you're face-to-face with someone, you have all five senses to engage in effective commu-nication and are therefore making a true connection.

Every degree to which you remove yourself from the face-to-face situation, the further you decrease the *quality* of the connection to the person you're communicating with, until it becomes almost meaningless and you might as well be sending a mass text message.

This means that the best way to network is—and always will be—getting out there and meeting people face-to-face. This also means that you will need to first identify who (generally speak-ing) you need to be networking with and then find a way to be where they are—whether it's an industry event, a charity event, an organization they attend, a class being taught by an expert in your field, whatever. You will always have to make the effort; rarely will anyone who can actually be of help to you magically come to you on their own. They simply have better things to do.

Rule 12: Start networking like a dog!

The You Brand

THE INTERNET HAS changed everything for entertainers. It has directly and instantaneously made it possible to connect your art and even you—yourself—to the world. Whether you're a musician, actor, filmmaker, writer, director, comedian, voice-over artist, anything, artists now have the ability to reach everyone and anyone with an Internet connection with the push of a button. The Internet is also like a bulldozer. While a bulldozer is capable of doing extremely powerful things, like clear a forest, it also kills a lot of things in the process. What the Internet gives in power, it takes away with privacy.

As with anything, with more access comes more responsibility, a truism that's perhaps never been more important than with the relatively new ability to expose yourself to the entire world simply by hitting send.

It's very wise to take this responsibility seriously since we, as artists and people in public view, have only one really good opportunity to create a positive and desirable brand for ourselves. Private things being made public (that wouldn't have even been possible to expose twenty years ago) have damaged and even destroyed many great careers. We see it on the news almost daily, in fact, whether it's actors, singers, athletes, politicians, or anyone in the public sphere "outed" for some action or other violation of the public moral code.

The Invisible People

But what we never hear about are the stories of the millions of "almost-beens" who lost their chance of a brilliant career as a result of poor branding early on. I've met a lot of them and have even worked with a few . . . briefly! I hope I can keep you from being one of them by pointing out some very simple rules to follow.

What Is Branding?

In their book *The Twenty-Two Immutable Laws of Branding,* Al Ries and Laura Ries describe what branding does: "From the [show] business point of view, branding in the marketplace is very similar to branding on the ranch. A branding program should be designed to differentiate your cow [you] from all the other cattle on the range."

Before I go into what good branding and brand management looks like, let me elaborate a little bit more on what bad branding can do. The kiss of death for any entertainer is becoming a tabloid joke. It can take only seconds, and all your hard-earned applause will turn to gawking. Once gawking sets in, your fifteen-minute clock starts ticking.

Sadly, the phrase "There's no such thing as bad publicity" has stuck around from the old days, back before there was even such a thing as Internet access, YouTube, and camera/video phones.

Back then, a well-placed "scandal" could often even reinvigorate a career for one simple reason: it could be carefully managed and be creatively spun by a handful of people holding all of the power, people who were able to easily control the flow of information. Newspapers, tabloids, and even broadcasters could be bought off and/or wined and dined, and favors could be cashed in, all in the name of tabloid advertising dollars, just so long as it all ended up smelling like roses for the entertainer in the end.

That classic quid pro quo, thanks to technology, has now and forever been reduced to 100 percent quid. There are no gatekeepers anymore who are capable of completely undoing what you alone can do in one nanosecond online or anywhere the camera-phone wielding public can see you.

Unfortunately, tabloid-style notoriety has become a classic trap for the eager entertainer, because (like any drug) fame that gets mistaken for applause can seem like a shortcut to happiness. Trust me when I tell you that no matter how they pretend to react to being "caught with their pants down," these celebs always lose in the end; even if they don't lose their career, they always lose their dignity.

Sure, the industry can be forgiving—if and only if:

- You've already proven yourself
- You've already made a lot of other people money and are still capable of making them a lot more money in the future
- You're smart enough to come clean quickly—at least making it *appear* that you have learned your lesson

These things will not, however, repair your dignity and your now-permanent reputation as a joke, quack, addict, idiot, or jerk. You merely just turned a respectable career into a working version of these things.

What Matters

This simply means that every social media networking post, every blog, every tweet, every picture taken of you, and every video posted of you matters. It all ads up to the You Brand and will either help you or hurt you; rarely will it do both.

From the beginning of my career, I made a conscious decision to never knowingly pose for a picture while doing anything that could be interpreted as even somewhat unacceptable to the most conservative fan. I figure, why chance turning even one potential fan or employer away from me?

While I can't control every picture taken of me, you'll still never see me post a controversial picture or video of myself. Sadly that's just the opposite of what seems to be happening in this fame-obsessed world these days, with some even releasing sex tapes of themselves!

But for you, the conscientious career-minded entertainer, this is all good news. Why? Mark Twain's words are worth repeating here: "Let us be thankful for the fools; but for them the rest of us could not succeed."

How to Make Sure Branding Works for You

Branding is a social science. It can be measured and tested, and there are a few unbreakable laws for branding success, as beautifully diagrammed by Al Ries and his daughter Laura in *The Twenty-Two Immutable Laws of Branding*. Their laws apply extremely well to entertainment, even though they were originally written primarily for selling manufactured products. Of course, as you already know and as I've stated earlier, *you* are the product you're selling.

Based on my own experience, I have synthesized these laws into the seven entertainment-specific principles of branding. Use these seven principles to carefully create and manage your You Brand!

The Seven Immutable Principles of Entertainment Branding

Principle One: K.I.S.S. (Keep It Simple, Stupid)—You Can't Be All Things to Everyone!

The fastest way to confuse a potential employer in entertainment is to do what I did when I first started out. I wanted everyone to know that I believed I could do just about anything in entertainment, and I would often tell them as much. I even had a business card that said "Evan Farmer—Diversified Performer."

What this industry dictates, and what I learned very quickly, is that the people doing the hiring want a single artist doing a single profession. That doesn't mean you have to choose only one art, just that you have to *label* yourself as one thing at a time. This also speaks to the importance of maintaining focus.

In other words, consider each skill that you have to be a separate product or brand of its own. For me, this meant that if I was at an acting audition I would call myself an actor, at a hosting audition I would be a host, and so on for singing, modeling, etc. I have a completely different resume and a completely different reel for each of my labels, and I try not to let them overlap if I can help it.

Carrie Underwood won *American Idol* in 2005 and went on to become one of the small handful of winners to have any lasting success. One of the reasons she was able to do this was because she immediately branded herself exclusively as a country artist.

A friend of mine in Nashville who is a well-known drive-time DJ at a major pop radio station told me that despite his repeated requests and despite his studio being in the same building as a major country station, Carrie Underwood would frequently walk down the hall, past his door, to the country radio station. She consciously resisted the lure of having more publicity for the pay-off of being extremely focused in her branding. And it has clearly paid off for her!

The easiest way to adhere to this principle is to be sure that you can always provide a quick—one sentence—and very specific answer to the question "What do you do?"

Principle Two: Authenticity, in Two Parts—Never Make False Claims About Yourself, and Never Use Cheap Gimmicks to Get Noticed.

The best way to get noticed is to keep showing up, while the quickest way to ensure you never get invited back is to either make claims you can't back up or use a cheap gimmick to get noticed in the first place. Both are inauthentic, and everyone hates posers!

The bottom line is that people are suspicious of anyone claiming anything these days, no matter how big or small, so don't bother bragging and save yourself the step of having to prove skeptics wrong down the road. Instead, simply show up and entertain them . . . a lot. Let other people do all the bragging for you and, as a result, your brand will be authentic.

Another reality I learned from experience, one that you can exploit to your advantage, is this: entertaining people frequently is sometimes just as good as being the *best* entertainer. Familiarity is a powerful tool. I booked my first national commercial in New York after no fewer than a hundred auditions. That same month I booked three more. Moreover, every single person I know who's done the commercial audition circuit has had the exact same experience.

Why? This was mostly a result of the casting directors becoming familiar with me, not because I was all of a sudden doing something radically different in the audition room. They had simply become very comfortable with me.

Above all, let your audience speak for you! It's the reason you hear advertisements say, "but don't take our word for it!" These companies know, correctly, that their word isn't worth the paper it's written on or the device on which it was recorded. Instead, these companies bank on their authentic actions, as should you!

Principle Three: Alignment—Keep Great Company!

Whether you like it or not, you will eventually draw comparisons between yourself and other artists. The best way to make sure you are aligned with someone at the top of his or her game is to do the aligning yourself.

Make it known that you admire certain people and then emulate their best qualities publicly, both onstage and off.

Are they philanthropic? Funny? Humble? Mysterious? Generous with praise for others? Constantly trying to improve themselves? Be quick to give your role models credit for helping to shape your values, and people will respect you for it.

But be careful: the opposite also holds true. Align yourself with negative people through your actions, and you will become associated with all of their negative qualities, regardless if you share them all or not!

Principle Four: Accessibility—Why Buy the Cow When You Can Get the Milk for Free?

This is dangerous ground. You must strike a balance between being accessible and remaining an interesting commodity, retaining some degree of mystery. If faced with the choice, always err on the side of remaining a mystery.

In my bartending days I learned a saying, "You can always add more liquor to a drink, but you can't take it out once it's in the mix. Pour shy!" When it comes to publicity, you can always put yourself out there a little more, but it's hard to make yourself and especially any of your regrettable actions forgettable. Only time away (often a lot of time) can cure over-exposure.

It's so ridiculously easy to make ourselves accessible via computers and mobile devices these days that we run the risk of mistaking this access with it being a good thing. It's the "everyone's doing it" trap.

I personally shudder when I see artists out there (well-intentioned, but still) seeking an audience by letting the world into their private lives to a huge extent. As I type, there are any number of ways that folks, celebrities included, have created a virtual real-time reality show by exposing their personal lives through social media at the expense of becoming yesterday's flavor of the month. This only ends up making that person less interesting, because everyone already knows or feels like they know everything about them!

I recently read that a major reason for the tremendous decline in popularity of the late-night talk shows relates to the fact that viewers no longer have to tune in in order to see a clever host trick a celebrity into revealing juicy facts about themselves. This is simply because many stars these days are giving you whatever information you want, whenever you want it, online already. The result is that they've effectively reduced the value of their own biggest commodity—their brand! This is a crystal clear example of what's meant by the phrase: "Why buy the cow when you can get the milk for free?"

Yes, you need to take advantage of all the latest technology has to offer, but you also need to make sure it's working *for* your brand, as being overexposed can actually be far worse than being ever-present!

If you do find yourself overexposed, however, don't worry too much; it's never too late to repair most of the damage, it just takes time. Simply stop what you're doing, pull back, and wait. People will eventually be curious again. It's human nature.

Final Note: I sincerely hope that it's also obvious why the storied "casting couch" could never benefit your career for exactly the same reasons! It is my greater hope that you're never faced with such a (thankfully uncommon) solicitation.

Principle Five: Consistency

You may not always be an actor, TV host, composer, writer, dancer, or singer throughout the course of your career, but you can and should remain extremely consistent in the other critical areas that will follow you around for the rest of your life. These include such things as integrity, being on time, remembering names, being professional, being prepared to work, never complaining, and under-promising and over-delivering, for example.

Furthermore, like those who hire you, when someone pays to see or hear your work, they will want to know what they're getting ahead of time. If you fail to consistently produce a quality performance, they'll stop paying—no one wants to chance wasting their hard-earned money.

Sadly, just turn on the news and you'll see any number of artists being paraded in and out of court and/or addiction treatment centers. Some have become so erratic and so professionally inconsistent that they have made themselves virtually unemployable despite their natural talent and abilities.

For the few artists who have managed to become big enough stars despite their erratic behavior, production companies are often required (by the financiers) to purchase multimillion-dollar insurance policies to guarantee that the project won't lose its investment capital if the artist doesn't perform up to standard, gets arrested, becomes incapacitated, or dies before the project is completed. In either case, the entertainer's career ends predictably quickly.

Principle Six: Publicity—It Should Only Be Used to Promote!

This principle comes after Accessibility since, by now, I would hope that you agree that in this day and age, not all publicity is good publicity.

Too often, people view publicity as a popularity contest with the purpose of stroking their ego and making themselves feel good. There are many reasons that this is a dangerous practice, but the bottom line is that this type of "needy" motivation always ends up muddying your image and therefore your brand.

The public today is very savvy and will spot your insecurities a mile away. And insecurities are, generally speaking, not pretty things. With this in mind, any brand-minded publicity effort should have only two goals (which should always be focused on positive promotion): to drive people to support a specific project, and to reinforce your personal unique brand image.

While you're busy distinguishing yourself as something truly unique and desirable, always keep in mind that it's critical to leave the public wanting more (maintaining the mystery).

Johnny Depp is a great example of how to do this. He's enjoyed one of the most celebrated acting careers, in some part as a result of his ability to remain available yet elusive and interesting yet relatively tabloid free. Above all, he's a celebrity whose personal life is still almost a complete mystery after nearly three decades of high-profile work!

Consistency is also critical to publicity. It's in the media that you can quickly become branded a liar, a hypocrite, or a fake if the public spots any inconsistency. Just ask any singer caught lip-syncing or the "wholesome" celebrity caught cheating on a spouse.

Whatever you want your reputation to be, you must be prepared to be consistent with it in all publicity endeavors that you engage in and be prepared to back it up, even when you're not onstage or in front of the camera. This is perhaps the harshest reality of a high-profile career in entertainment today: the near total and utter loss of privacy.

Principle Seven: Entertain—It Helps to Be Good at Your Craft, But It's Critical to Be Able to Entertain!

Entertainment can be described as "pleasant distraction." People are often willing to pay you massive sums of money if you can make them forget about their problems for a while and feel good in the meantime. At the risk of being overly redundant, this has relatively little to do with talent or skill at a particular craft itself. Some of the most entertaining actors never acquire the ability to disappear into their role, just like some of the most entertaining singers are often fairly limited vocally. That doesn't change the fact that they might be among the best entertainers in their field, a singular craft unto itself.

I have never been, or even claimed to be, the best at any of the entertainment professions I've successfully worked in, but I have always done *one thing* fairly successfully over and over: I have always been able to entertain people consistently, and that is one of the things I'm known for.

Your professional title may be actor, singer, comedian, film director, whatever. But your *brand* should always include: "great entertainer."

Rule 13: Consciously choose to create and control your brand early with The Seven Immutable Principles of Entertainment Branding.

PART V

ACTION

ADMIT ONE

Successful people . . . do all the things unsuccessful people don't want to do, like staying enthusiastic when you keep on getting rejected.

—JOHN PAUL DEJORIA, BILLIONAIRE COFOUNDER OF
PAUL MITCHELL HAIR PRODUCTS AND PATRÓN SPIRITS

At the beginning of this book, I made the assertion that *Breaking In* is based on two overall theorems for success that I have seen played out in life and in research over and over again, and they are:

Successful people think differently than unsuccessful people.

Successful people work harder than unsuccessful people.

The three previous sections of the book, Think, Traits, and Skills, concentrated on areas specific to the mind that must be addressed and mastered if you want to have the edge for success in this industry and in life. This last section, which addresses one single component of success, Action, or the "working harder" component for success, is in my opinion the most important one in the book.

Why? Because you can have the most brilliantly trained mind in the world, yet without taking action, *nothing* happens. Perhaps more amazingly though, it's also entirely possible to have a completely untrained mind but still find success just by taking massive action! I think few people would argue that there are plenty of über-successful people in entertainment who also have some real psychological issues and deficiencies. They just took a massive amount of action, the kind that most average people don't want to take to get there.

The 100/20/1 Rule

The one and only thing that all consistently successful people have in common is that all of them took far more action than their unsuccessful counterparts. They not only did more, but they were all willing to do all of the things that other people simply weren't willing to do.

In order to get a single job in entertainment, you will be well served to embrace what I call the 100/20/1 rule:

> **It takes 100 auditions to get 20 callbacks (second auditions) to get 1 job.**

Depending on where you are in your career, those numbers will vary. For example, I went to no fewer than three hundred auditions to get a handful of callbacks to get my first entertainment job in New York City. These days, depending on the kind of job I'm after, it could be twenty auditions to get the callback that lands me the job. Even major stars don't get every job they want, and in most cases they still have to audition and fight like hell to get the jobs they do want! A great example of this is Rob Lowe's description of his fight to win the role of Sam Seaborn on the hit series *The West Wing* (for which he was nominated for an Emmy and two Golden Globe Awards), as told in his book *Stories I Only Tell My Friends.*

Throughout my career, and still to this day, I'll very often see huge stars sitting outside casting offices waiting to audition just like everyone else. Kristin Chenoweth, in her brilliant memoir *A Little Bit Wicked,* talks about bumping into Oscar winner Patty Duke at a TV pilot audition and finding out later that Patty didn't even get the part she auditioned for! As Kristin points out, "You can have an Oscar and it doesn't mean jack!"

The point is that it's always going to be a numbers game, no matter how talented or famous you are, because there will always be other people who are just as talented and famous or even non-famous (frequently, as in Rob Lowe's case with *The West Wing,* they were initially looking for "unknowns") who want that same job and will be willing to go that extra mile to get it. This means that you will have to go an extra, extra, extra mile if you want to have a really good shot at it. This is what John Paul DeJoria is talking about in the opening quote of this section.

Other things that successful people are willing to do that many unsuccessful ones are not willing to do include:

- Maintaining enthusiasm after a hundred rejections in a row
- Keeping at it for ten years or more until you get your break
- Waking up at 4:00 a.m. every day to rehearse, research, exercise, etc.
- Working or rehearsing long after everyone else goes home
- Living way beneath your means in order to have the money to invest in your career
- Working at less than glamorous subsistence jobs to get by
- Doing work for no pay in exchange for the experience
- Taking risks that terrify most people
- Breaking ties with disfunctional yet comfortable relationships
- Expecting far more from yourself than anyone will ever expect from you
- Being extremely lonely at times

This list could go on and on and be a book of its own. The point is, if you aren't willing and able to do these types of things, not only is success in entertainment highly unlikely for you, but you're likely headed for nothing more than mediocrity in whatever you do in life. That's harsh but very realistic news. And for some people that is perfectly OK.

Here's the good news: As I've already stated, you don't need to have a brilliant mind to succeed. You could literally do the opposite of everything in the previous three sections of this book, and yet still succeed off the charts by just being off the charts in the action department. Some of it will be luck, some of it will be wasted action, but in the end you can still succeed just by simply taking more action and by doing the necessary things that average people refuse to do. People may call you crazy—many who succeed this way probably are—but you'll still succeed.

The second piece of good news is that you don't have to be crazy in order to be willing and able to do all of the necessary things that unsuccessful people aren't! That's where the previous sections of this book come in, and it's why I put them in this order. All you need in order to take the kind of action necessary for enormous success in this industry is to have a realistic understanding of what success in entertainment requires. Specifically, this means you need to acquire the thinking habits, traits, and skills of the most successful people who came before you. It's a simple task, but one that requires a lot of work.

With that foundation, action is likely to be inevitable, since your conscience will hold you accountable to this information. After all, once you know what needs to be done, you'll either want success enough to do those things, or you will always know that it could have been yours if you had only done them. A conscience never lies.

Now all you need to do is ratchet your actions up to extreme actions and you'll be unstoppable. That's what this section is all about.

ACTION 1:

The Part Nike Left Out—The Power of Three

Twenty years from now you will be more disappointed by the things that you didn't do than by the ones you did do. . . . Sail away from the safe harbor. Catch the trade winds in your sails. Explore. Dream. Discover.

—MARK TWAIN

It's easy to get pumped up from reading a book, attending a particularly motivating seminar, or even seeing a powerful movie like *Rocky* and decide, "I'm going to kick _ss, and nothing's going to stop me!"—and then suddenly find yourself deflated and not knowing where to start. In fact, this experience can even have a negative effect, because it can easily lead to the feeling that you've let yourself down. In business consulting circles, they call this the "Seminar Effect." In everyday life, this manifests itself in feeling overwhelmed.

As discussed in chapter 12, Using Emotional Alchemy to Get Work, whenever you feel overwhelmed, you need to stop and reprioritize. When it comes to taking extreme action (a reference to volume, not extreme risk), the kind that differentiates between people who remain average and those who become a superstar, you not only need to have your priorities in order, but you need to start with the small actions first. This builds momentum without psyching you out in the meantime. As Martin Luther King, Jr., said: "You don't have to see the whole staircase. Just take the first step."

Back to the Beginning

In 1988, a man named Dan Wieden, cofounder of the Portland-based advertising agency Wieden+Kennedy, coined perhaps one of the most famous and celebrated ad slogans ever created for his client, the Nike shoe company: *Just Do It.*

As a worshipper of all things simple, I fell in love with this phrase and everything it represented in three little words. Like many of the billions of people who would eventually hear or see those words associated with Nike, I was pumped up. I felt like I now had three magic words that would take me from hesitation and doubt straight into the arms of awe-inspiring action. Or did I?

By the time I arrived in New York in 1995, that genius, three-word slogan was plastered next to just about every picture of a Nike shoe, just about everywhere you looked. I came to view those three words, Just Do It, as a sign from the heavens and even, to some degree, as my own personal calling card.

After all, I was ambitious if nothing else. I may not have known how I was going to attain my goal of a career in film, television, music, print, and stage, but all of a sudden I didn't seem to need to know, I could Just Do It.

Then my alarm clock went off that first morning, and I woke up overwhelmed and paralyzed by the enormity of my ambition. I realized that the big it, the same one I figured I would *just do,* was the size of Mount Everest. I was at its metaphorical base camp: naked, out of shape, and without a sherpa. I wasn't going to *just do* anything.

The romance of that sweet slogan wore off quickly, and

after attempting to fix the problem by adding my own addition, *Just Do It . . . Anyway*—even inscribing those four words, ellipses and all, onto the back of my iPod, I realized that I not only needed to set some realistic expectations, but I needed to figure out exactly what those people who climbed—or even moved—mountains did first to accomplish their task. In other words, I really needed a sherpa.

So once again, I looked to the great achievers of all time (the best sherpas available) for advice; and the answer turned out to be simpler than I thought: the first act of moving a mountain is to pick up a shovel.

Every single monumental achievement ever accomplished started with a series of *small* accomplishments that eventually snowballed into that one *big* thing.

Thomas Edison had no fewer than ten thousand of them before the lightbulb worked. The Wright brothers didn't take on gravity; but they did take on the few engineering tasks that they could handle each day until they flew.

Imagine waking up one day in the early 1900s and saying, "I'm going to create light" or "I'm going to be the first to fly!" That approach would stop any reasonable person from ever even starting; the same way saying, "I'm going to be the most successful artist to ever live" stops many extremely talented people from ever starting. But then Edison, the Wright brothers, and most superstars didn't do that; they focused on the small tasks, and that was their secret.

As I mentioned at the beginning of this book, success starts in the mind and, in this case, it all starts with perspective.

The trick I realized shortly after beginning my journey up the side of the great entertainment mountain was to not worry about the giant ice-covered vertical wall I faced but to concentrate on what I could do now. I had to concentrate on the baby steps first—i.e., setting that first "ice screw."

For me, at the start of my career, I could do a few things:

1. Move to New York City or Los Angeles.
2. Get a subsistence job.
3. Read everything I could about the first steps guys like Tom Cruise, Rob Lowe, and Harrison Ford took toward their careers.

> Even the largest tree can be felled with three swings of an axe each day.
> —*Proverb*

4. Put together a headshot and résumé.
5. Get on the phone and cold call talent agencies, acquaintances, family friends, friends of friends, friends of friends of acquaintances in New York who might know people in any branch of the entertainment business, and ask them a million questions.
6. Hunt down trade papers listing auditions and mail a headshot and résumé to each one.
7. Take a few classes and ask a million questions.

I made a rule for myself: I would do three career-oriented things everyday . . . no matter what. For example, on day one I did the following:

- Applied for a bartending job.
- Called a photographer to set up headshots.
- Read an interview with Harrison Ford.

I could do more if I wanted on any given day, but I allowed myself to stop stressing about progress after the first three things were done, and I'd pat myself on the back for succeeding that day. Sometimes I even celebrated by splurging on the fancy kind of Ramen Noodles!

After a little experimenting, I found that one or two actions were not enough. Requiring that third task of myself forced me to stretch just enough each day. On the other hand, requiring more than three tasks from myself turned me into a basket case and made me feel like a failure when I fell short. This only served to diminish any hard-earned confidence and momentum I had built up. That was a risk I couldn't afford to take.

Three tasks per day was always doable—even on the craziest of days—and it allowed me to sleep at night. Three tasks is also enough to build up momentum, which more often than not leads to accomplishing far more than just three goals anyway.

Starting out in New York, my life looked a lot like this: The first week it felt like I applied to every bartending job available in the city (at least three a day). By week two I was working four nights a week at the one place that hired me.

Every day that I wasn't working, I'd march down to the public library or bookstore and scour copies of *Biography* magazine for articles and interviews with the most successful names in entertainment as well as any other book I could find that might offer success tips. Nowadays my march down to the library is often replaced by a march to my home office to do a focused, undistracted, search on the web.

Once at the library or bookstore, I made myself do one of two things before I was allowed to leave: find one useful book and read it or read at least three different interviews or stories about the careers of people I wanted to emulate. Sometimes that would take me all day; often it would only be a couple of hours. Then I'd go have some fun.

Through this process, I was learning, *in their own words,* how people like Oprah Winfrey, Johnny Depp, Harrison Ford, Angelina Jolie, Will Smith, Madonna, Bono, Brad Pitt, and Tom Hanks got their start. From them I pieced together what I needed to do next, which was to get an agent. As I've already described, that process took me about three months.

With an agent representing me, I went from going to trade-paper auditions (bottom rung) to exclusive top-rung auditions for major commercials, major films, major TV shows, major plays, major modeling "go-sees," and auditions for major record labels. These were the auditions where I'd regularly compete with guys like Zach Braff *(Scrubs),* Edward Norton *(Primal Fear),* and Matthew Morrison *(Glee).*

The Rube Goldberg Effect

Once you start taking a lot of action (no fewer than three each day), something magical happens. You start to see things come together that at first glance seemed to have nothing to do with each other. Opportunities seem to appear out of thin air. I call this the Rube Goldberg effect.

Rube Goldberg, an American cartoonist, sculptor, author, engineer, and inventor, became famous for his wild contraptions in which one action—for example, tipping over a single domino—triggers another series of actions, until a completely unrelated goal is accomplished. For example: The domino may trigger a switch that allows a boot to swing on a pendulum, that kicks a basketball onto a track, that drops into a bucket, that pulls a string, that is attached to a light switch, that turns on a light. You get the idea.

The significance of this metaphor isn't that it would have been easier to just skip the steps and simply walk across the room to turn on the light, because in life that's not always possible. Sometimes all we have at our disposal at any given moment is that single domino that starts it all.

The beauty of it is that even though the domino may not initially appear to have anything to do with the light switch, once you knock it over, the chain reaction you set in motion collects all of these seemingly random parts and manifests an impressive result. And as long as each of those parts merely shares the same basic motivation—namely, to achieve your entertainment career goal—the result you get is very often exactly the one you're looking for.

A prime example of how this worked in my life was the way in which I came to MTV's attention for the casting of the movie *2GE+HER*. Before going to Russia to tour with the band Ha-Ha, I had auditioned to host a new show at MTV called *Total Request Live*. (Ultimately, the job went to Carson Daly, who was a radio DJ at the time.)

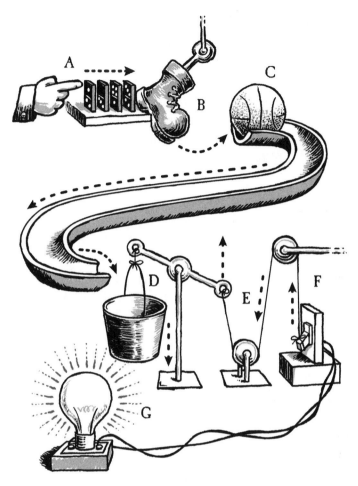

Several months after I returned from Russia, a record label exec I had met with about recording an album mentioned my name to the head of MTV casting. That casting director remembered me from the hosting audition and called my agent to see if I was also an actor, at which point he discovered I was in the middle of filming my first movie, *Shaft Returns.*

Here was a case in which my actions in three completely different career genres—hosting, singing, and acting—came together for a unique opportunity.

If landing this role was the metaphorical Rube Goldberg "light being turned on," I would likely never have gotten there without first auditioning to host an MTV show (the falling domino), then taking a job touring with the Russian band Ha-Ha (the swinging boot), which then led to my meeting with a record producer (the basketball on a track), who then mentioned my name to the head of casting, who remembered me from the hosting audition (the dropping bucket), who decided to call me in to screen-test for the role (string attached to the light switch), which ultimately led to me getting a career-changing role (the light)!

And for each of those individual things that led to that role, there was an equal number of seemingly unrelated actions that I took that led to them. This is the magic of the Rube Goldberg effect, which is the result of taking massive action.

Though it took four years to arrive at the first peak of my career, by just taking no fewer than three actions a day toward my career goals, I found myself at the top of a once seemingly unclimbable mountain with a couple of stadium tours, a couple of films, a couple of gold albums, and more opportunities to come.

So, what did Nike leave out? What "it" should be. And that is: *Just Do . . . Three Things Every Day.* It's that simple. With the addition of this new phrase, the meaning changes from "Just . . . get off your butt, you lazy slob and do something!" to "Just . . . do three things today and you're solid!"

That's the successful way of thinking: a subtle, yet crucial, distinction. One phrase punishes you; the other sets clear parameters and rewards you. One phrase calls you names if and when you don't succeed, and the other phrase very much wants you to win.

They call this first scenario "setting yourself up for failure," but since, as you remember, the successful mind doesn't acknowledge the concept of *failure,* we won't be going there anyway. This new phrase simply adds insurance, and now you're setting yourself up for *success.*

So What Should You Do First?

By now I think you already know my answer. It comes directly from the mouths of the Angelina Jolies, the Spielbergs, the Lady Gagas, the Oprah Winfreys, the Bonos, the Baryshnikovs (think of the biggest name in your particular field) of the world.

What did *they* do first? While you may not get the first three tasks toward your goals from one person (for example, Oprah had some very unique challenges that you may not relate to), it's fairly easy to piece together a good place to start by researching the careers of several different über-successful people in your field.

These people, who are at the top of their game, are also your number-one place to return to if you ever get stuck, make a mistake, or just feel like you're in a rut. They've been there too, and they not only got through it, but they also went on to become among the best in history. I personally choose their advice over Uncle Steven's because, unless your uncle happens to be Steven Spielberg and you also happen to be an aspiring filmmaker, they—more than anyone else in the world—know how to succeed at their craft!

An important thing to remember is the rule *as if*. It's often just as good to imagine what actions that person *would have taken* or would take in your current situation as it is to find an example of when they faced your exact obstacle. In these cases, just take action as if you were them!

The true value that comes from studying the über-successful is the internalizing of their instincts and values, which comes from learning and understanding their actions in general over the course of their careers.

So the next time you're stuck, just ask yourself: What would Brad Pitt do? Or: What would Lady Gaga do? And then take that action yourself.

Rule 14: Just Do . . . Three Things Toward Your Career Goal Every Day!

ACTION 2:

The Most Important Action You Will Ever Take

A RESEARCHER NAMED Dr. Lewis Terman at Stanford University conducted a study with the intention of finding a correlation between IQ and success. He ultimately demonstrated that a person's IQ was *not* the most critical component of success.

After following 1,500 children with IQs at the genius level for several decades, Dr. Terman found just three factors to be the largest single determiners of success: self-confidence, perseverance, and the ability to set goals.

You may also recall the study cited in Chapter 4 that showed that a key distinguishing variable for the success of musicians was not natural talent but rather that they worked much, much harder than their less-successful colleagues. In other words, the insatiable musicians persevered through boredom and frustration and became successful.

Unlike IQ or natural artistic talent, anyone can become confident and insatiable, though it may require a lot of effort practicing techniques like those described in previous chapters.

Goal-setting, on the other hand, the last of Dr. Terman's three key determinants of success, is an absolute no-brainer. But most unsuccessful people don't do it. Why? While there are probably any number of reasons, depending on the person, I can tell you why I was reluctant to do it as part of a class assignment in college. The main reason was that I simply couldn't see how goal-setting, the actual sit-down-and-do-it side of the process, was any different from knowing what I wanted in my head.

I can also tell you how this little distinction changed my life and is a key factor in how I have been able to do what I have done in my life, and it is why I call this chapter The Most Important Action You Will Ever Take!

A Begrudging Assignment

During my final semester before graduating, the professor of a class called Organizational Issues Management, a study of what makes a company successful, had us each write out a list of ten goals: four six-month goals, four ten-year goals, and two long-term before-you-die goals.

At that moment, I remember thinking, well, I want to be rich and famous—what could possibly be the point of writing that down, much less anything beyond that?

Sitting in my room that night, I realized that what I found so intimidating about writing out my specific goals was that I instinctively knew that it was akin to signing a contract with myself. Once I wrote the specific goals down, I was on the hook for doing whatever it took to achieve them, and that was a lot of pressure I didn't think I wanted or needed. Once written, I instinctively also knew I'd never allow myself to settle for close-enough either.

The second urge I had to fight was the urge to make them all easy to obtain so that I would feel less pressure and anxiety.

Difficult goals consistently lead to higher performance than easy goals or simply "trying to do your best." My professor knew this, and we were assured that our list of goals would be carefully vetted and our grade would reflect the relative sincerity of our efforts. After struggling for several hours and consuming a few frozen pizzas, I managed to squeeze out the following list of goals:

Short Term (Six-Month) Goals:

1. Appear in a national commercial.
2. Appear as a model in a major print ad.
3. Perform a lead role in a respected stage production.
4. Graduate from college *cum laude.*

Long Term (Ten-Year) Goals:

1. Gain representation by a major talent agent in either New York or LA.
2. Star in a major motion picture.
3. Star in a TV series.
4. Hear a song I recorded on the radio.

Ultimate (Before I Die) Goals:

1. Be able to live comfortably as an entertainment professional.
2. Have a happy and healthy family including a wife and at least one child.

Considering that at the time I had absolutely zero professional experience in any of those fields, my goals were undeniably difficult and lofty. Nonetheless, I ended up achieving every one of them, and I did so pretty much in that exact order.

Within six months of creating the list, I had appeared in a national Mountain Dew commercial, I was featured on a billboard all over New Orleans in an advertisement for a Daiquiris chain, I appeared as the lead role of "Chip" in Tulane Summer Lyric's production of *On the Town,* and then I graduated *cum laude.* And yes, I got an A in the class too.

I managed to accomplish my ten-year goals in only five, and just fifteen years later, I found myself able to live comfortably with entertainment as my full-time profession. Today I have a loving wife and two incredible sons.

Over the years, I've since modified, added to, and eliminated many of my goals hundreds of times, but I still do the exercise at least twice a year in order to update my goals. Yes, I write them out each time! These days I put the goals on my electronic calendar, and every Monday morning a current list pops up on my computer screen at 9:00 a.m.

Had I not physically forced myself to write these goals down in college (even if only to pass that class), I would never have made that contract with myself, and I would have probably only ever had a vague sense of what I wanted in my life and only a vague sense of accomplishment. More importantly, I would never have learned how effective it really is. In all likelihood, I would have been destined to end up with an average existence along with a huge side of disappointment and regret. That's where most people end up, but it is certainly not the domain of successful entertainers.

Here's a quick summary of how the mechanics of goal-setting works, according to psychologist Edwin A. Locke of the University of Maryland, considered to be one of the leading researchers in the area of motivation, leadership, and the power of goal-setting. The four goal mechanisms are as follows:

1. Goals serve a direct function; they direct attention and effort toward goal-relevant activities and away from goal-irrelevant activities.
2. Goals have an energizing function. High goals lead to greater efforts than low goals.
3. Goals affect persistence. When participants are allowed to control the time they spend on a task, hard goals prolong effort.
4. Goals affect action indirectly related to the arousal, discovery, and/or use of task-relevant knowledge and strategies. In

other words, every time you learn something related to your goal, you automatically tend to take *even more* action based on that information.

A completely fabricated Yale University study in 1953 (Yale has confirmed it does not exist) is frequently cited by motivational speakers regarding written goals. According to the nonexistent study, researchers surveyed Yale's graduating seniors to determine how many of them had specific, written goals for their future. The answer: 3 percent. Twenty years later, researchers polled the surviving members of the class of 1953 and found that the 3 percent who had written goals had accumulated more personal financial wealth than the other 97 percent of the class combined.

The mythical Yale study became so pervasive that eventually, several real studies were conducted, including one at Dominican University by Gail Matthews in 2002. What Dr. Matthews and the other studies have all found was that though the exact percentages vary slightly, the fictitious Yale study's premise was essentially correct.

Fact: The physical act of writing goals down contributes exponentially in determining future success.

The SMART Process

The most well-known system for getting the most out of goal-setting is called the SMART process, cited by George T. Doran in the November 1981 issue of *Management Review* magazine. Ideally, your written list of short-term, long-term, and ultimate goals should meet the following criteria in order for them to be successful:

- Specific
- Measurable
- Attainable

- Relevant
- Time-bound

Specific

This is the what, who, and where of each goal. The more of these questions you can answer about each of your goals, the stronger your contract with yourself will be and the more likely you are to achieve them.

By now, you have probably begun exploring the ten questions all successful artists ask (see chapter 7) in depth. Writing your specific goals down according to these three time frames is your first step in effective goal-setting.

Measurable

If your goal is to mail out twenty headshots/résumés each day, it's easy to see how you did by simply counting the stamps at the end of the day.

This is true for more complex goals as well. Take my first six-month career goal in college for example: to appear in a national commercial. The process of achieving that goal required getting a local agent to represent me and send me out on commercial auditions. That was measurable. Then it required going to every audition I was submitted for; again, measurable.

Before I landed the national Mountain Dew commercial, I booked a few local commercials, which was a clear and measurable indicator that I was progressing. Then I finally achieved my goal and became a "Dew Dude" (actual title).

No matter how complex your goal is, you must have a way of acquiring feedback so that your progress can be measured. This lets you know where you stand and what still needs to be done.

Attainable

The key here is not whether you think that you can attain these goals *right now,* but whether or not they are ever attainable. This is why it's necessary to have short-term, long-term, and ultimate goals.

If all we ever did was to write down our ultimate goals, we'd never get started because they'd never seem realistic. But that is exactly what most people tend to do by default when they simply say, "I want to be rich and famous," and leave it at that. The key is creating a more realistic plan along the way to being rich and famous and defining exactly what rich and famous means to you.

For example, by the time I had appeared in a national commercial (short-term goal), the idea of appearing in a major motion picture (long-term goal) wasn't so outlandish after all. By the time I had appeared in a couple of films, the idea of living comfortably as an entertainment professional (ultimate goal) was not only reasonable, it seemed likely.

Jim Carrey's 1987 goal of earning $10 million for "acting services rendered" by Thanksgiving 1995, for example, was likely in his long-term goal category. I'm willing to bet his short-term goals involved other slightly more attainable feats such as getting an agent, booking a lead role in a film, and so on—not entirely unlike my own list.

Relevant

This is the big *why* of each goal—your purpose combined with the goal's purpose itself. If you don't have a strong enough reason for wanting each goal, it is not going to be relevant to you for very long. You also must identify how one goal is a stepping-stone to the others. When I made my list of short-term goals, I knew that only after I accomplished *them* would I have the tools necessary to go after the long-term goals. This makes each goal relevant to the next one and, therefore, far more likely to be achieved.

Time-Bound

The most important clause to any contract is the deadline. This not only makes measuring progress possible, but it is also one of life's best motivators. It's amazing what people can accomplish on April 14, the day before taxes are due, and you'll be amazed at what you will find yourself capable of when you've made a specific time-bound contract with yourself.

Often this works subconsciously, and this is one of the reasons why writing down your goals with a specific time frame is so effective. Your internal compass simply won't let you fail. Once again, it's human nature.

The Final Step

The final step to effective goal-setting is to simply keep doing it. Once you achieve a goal, you must replace it with either another goal from your long-term goals list or another goal you discovered you wanted along the way. Just be SMART about it and you'll be as surprised as I was at how the power to achieve something big lay in the simple yet powerful act of writing it down.

> **Rule 15: WRITE your goals in terms of *six months, ten years,* and *ultimate* following the SMART requirements of effective goal setting: Specific, Measurable, Attainable, Relevant, and Time-Bound.**

ACTION 3:

Build Your Entertainment Dream Team

REGARDLESS OF WHAT area of entertainment you focus on, this business requires a team just like any other successful business. The better your team, the better your career will be too. This does not mean that in order to have a successful career you need to be surrounded by the biggest names, like William Morris, Clive Davis, or Paramount. It simply means that you need to create a team that works well for you.

I've employed representatives to work on my behalf who also worked with names like Brad Pitt and Matt Damon; I also received very little of their attention. I've also had super-hungry team members who did more to further my career in a year than almost everyone else combined had accomplished in twenty years.

Your goal should be to create the most effective team you can at each stage of the game by finding people who are both hungry on your behalf and capable of getting the job done at the same time. The good news is that this group is far more accessible to someone starting out than the big names are. The bad news is that everyone else (the smart ones anyway) wants them too, and they can't represent everybody.

This last reality is also your first clue to locating the effective team members: just figure out where the other smart people are looking, and look there too.

Let's take a look at what a typical "support crew" for any working artist looks like. A solid team will likely be made up of people who fit into three basic categories: support system, professional services, and advisors.

Support System

Your support system can be anything from family, friends, a girlfriend/boyfriend, a spouse, or your church—there are no points for going it alone. It is possible—many have—but a good support system rooting for you unquestioningly no matter what happens will pick you back up and gently nudge you back into the ring. This is an enormous asset.

This is a really good time to get rid of dysfunctional relationships and learn to avoid getting into any more relationships that will only serve to work against you. Here are just a few of the "types" you should try to avoid:

- *Wounded Birds:* People who are constantly in need but never offer anything in return.
- *Scene Stealers:* Folks who are constantly undermining you out of some misguided form of competition in which you aren't even participating.
- *Distracters:* People who don't share your ambition and frequently attempt to derail you so that you can be their "fun buddy."
- *Rotten Family:* Anyone from immediate family to a boyfriend or girlfriend who tries to capitalize on the word *family* in order to undermine your goals for any reason. Any of the above people who use manipulation to get something from you that's not in your best interest to give would also fall into this category.

- *Salespeople:* People who are hard-selling you a fast ticket to success.

The Subsistence Job Social Trap

When starting out in this business, you will find any number of these toxic personality types working alongside you at a typical subsistence job. Being a struggling artist often comes with a lot of insecurities, and most of the people who fall into these dysfunctional categories become that way from an inability to deal constructively with these insecurities. In other words, since they can't face the fact that they're not 100 percent in control of their career, they'll try to control *you* in order to feel better.

Whether it's luring you into their "let's go out and party all the time" lifestyle (distracters) or playing with your head by spreading industry gossip (scene stealers), it all serves to pull your valuable energy away from your true goals. It usually happens before you even realize it, and if you find yourself spending more time managing your social or work relationships than your career, it's time for a change.

I had to quit my first decent-paying bartending job in New York at a restaurant that was entirely staffed by aspiring artists (some very talented). Unfortunately, they also happened to be a toxic mix of all of the above personalities that seemed intent on dragging me down. The job I finally found and settled on, by contrast, had nothing to offer in the way of an attractive lifestyle or any kind of drama I could be drawn into. It was a job that paid my bills, plain and simple, and I left it behind, including my coworkers, as soon as I clocked out.

The key is being aware that these distracting and potentially destructive relationships are out there and seem to be especially prevalent anywhere groups of people struggling toward the same goals exist in large numbers.

The Sub-Industry of Entertainment

The last on the list of personality types to avoid, the salesperson, carries with him a particular set of characteristics that can make him more dangerous than the others. These folks are capable of not only stealing your money and your valuable time but some are also capable of undermining your natural instincts and even confidence, all in the name of keeping you hooked, in order to keep you paying.

I call it the *sub-industry of entertainment.* For every dream out there, there exists a full-blown industry of people selling you a set of "tools" and "inside fast-tracks" to achieving that dream. I even see a few of them exposed by investigative journalists from time to time.

Once you know what to look for, some of these salespeople are fairly easy to spot from the ads: "Think you've got what it takes to be on TV and in movies? Then _____ Agency wants *you* to audition right here in your area!" Or the "modeling agencies" that send out "talent scouts" to malls all over the country who are trained at using flattery and other sales techniques to lure young kids and their parents into coughing up thousands of dollars for useless packages with false promises.

The sales pitch varies, but the common denominator always remains the same: they spot tremendous yet undeveloped natural talent in you, and *they* want *you* to pay *them* to show you the ropes. Whether they promise to represent you and your vast talent or beauty (always for a fee) or they promise to teach you the tricks of the trade that you absolutely have to know, just about all of them require training at their facility or acquiring expensive head-shots with their photographer; and trust me, their photographer ain't cheap.

Bottom line: there are far too many talented and qualified actors, singers, performers, models, you name it, who are *willing* to go to New York, Hollywood, or Nashville for there

**to be any motivation whatsoever for New York, Hollywood,
or Nashville to come to your town.**

Ask any reputable, union-monitored agent in the business,
and they'll tell you that anyone who is legit, someone who can
legitimately provide you access to real career opportunities,
will *never* ask you for money up front or require you to use their
school, photographer, etc. for a fee! If you truly have a marketable ability, a legitimate agent will make money *only* when
you make money. The reasoning is simple: qualified and reputable model and talent agents got to be reputable because casting directors and producers trust them to bring the best talent to
them while, at the same time, weeding out the rest—also known
as the "mall kids." All an agent would have to do to lose that
critical trust they depend on for their continued business would
be to send out just a few entirely ill-qualified candidates.

In addition, legitimate agencies are actually regulated by the
unions as a means of checks and balances to this end. In other
words, they aren't allowed to take money from you up front
even if they want to!

Some of the scam operations will even stage fake auditions
just to keep the carrot dangling out in plain sight and keep your
money rolling in. Those mentioned above are the most obvious
traps, but the rule of thumb to avoid them is simple: if someone
calling herself an agent or manager asks you for money up front,
she is bad news!

The Gray Area Industries

Salespeople types also lurk within the larger area of the sub-
industry of entertainment, in a place I call the gray areas of the
business. These are usually services that may be perfectly legit
in what they provide, but like any drug they can be dangerously
addictive and are inherently self-sustaining in nature, because
they play to your insecurities in order to establish an emotional
dependence on their product. What am I referring to? Specifi-

cally, the trade classes that every artist needs in order to learn his or her craft, whether it's acting, singing, dancing, comedy, or filmmaking.

You may remember me describing the experience I had with an acting teacher who actually asked me to sign a document stating that I agreed not to audition for any professional work until the two-year program was complete (at which point I suspect I'd be told that I still wasn't "ready" and be asked to sign another pledge keeping me in class even longer). You may also remember that I became a highly paid working actor the day after I quit the class when I auditioned for and booked a national commercial. This particular teacher may very well have been one of the salespeople who didn't even realize what they were doing consciously, and may have just been following the rules of the school she was working for, but whether she was the salesperson or the school was, the net effect was the same. And in case you were wondering, this is a very well-known acting school!

I'm not at all denouncing any and every training program that endorses such policies. For some artists, these policies are a good thing in that they provide a much-needed focus on the art before muddying the waters on the business side of things. For me, at that particular stage in my training and life, I needed to be focused more on the business.

Perhaps the most important thing to remember here is that any training you seek should be sought solely for the purpose of achieving your goal, which for the aspiring professional should be the goal of getting paid to work as soon as possible. And, as I mentioned before, a good rule of thumb to follow is that the minute you start to wonder if you're ready to focus on the business, it's time to jump.

After all, being the best entertainer in the world won't ever pay your bills if people don't pay to come to see you. And . . .

People won't pay to see your art unless you're employed doing it, and you won't get employed doing your art if you're

**not out there selling it. My advice is to seek teachers/train-
ers who also support this goal.**

I eventually found an acting instructor whose list of students reads like the Who's Who of Hollywood. Not only did she
end up being an excellent teacher, but with so many working
students she was also very knowledgeable and connected
within the working side of the business as well. This is the type
of resource you should look for.

Keep in mind that, in actual practice, I have always found
that the highest quality training you will ever receive is on-the-
job training!

Professional Services

You should immediately start researching the best available
professional services in your field. Even if they are currently out
of your reach, you need to know who and what the successful
people use to further their career. While there are any number of
specialty services out there, for the most part the following four
groups will likely forever be the foundation of any career in
entertainment.

Agents and Managers

When you're an entertainer with little work experience, it's
unlikely that the William Morris Agency or Sony Music Group
will start making calls on your behalf, but of course most of
their clients didn't start their careers there either. Until you
qualify for their attention, many people will seek out an inter-
mediate-level agency or manager that can help you get there.

As I mentioned earlier, there are any number of ways to
acquire an agent or manager, ranging from the traditional
method of inviting one to see you perform to the creative
process I used. How you go about it will all come down to your
current assets, the stage of your career, and your creativity. It's
worth repeating here that in any business, the personal recom-

mendation is always the most efficient means to get in the door. The only way to be the person who gets recommended is through effective networking.

Producers

It is becoming more and more common these days for music producers, television producers, and film producers to go out and find talented people themselves and develop them as a package deal with their specific project, which they then intend to sell to a larger production company, network, or record label. These are typically called development deals, and they follow a similar structure to the old "studio deals" that used to, for all intents and purposes, professionally own artists like Marilyn Monroe or Elvis Presley.

Seeking an up-and-coming producer in your field can be a great way to get the kind of work that attracts a top agent or manager.

Attorneys

Artists often find entertainment attorneys who also act as managers for their clients in addition to providing legal services. This is very common among stars with high net worth, especially in the music industry, but this relationship has also been known to exist with up-and-comers as well. This was the primary relationship from the beginning between attorney Larry Rudolph and his clients Britney Spears, Justin Timberlake, 98 Degrees, The Backstreet Boys, Jessica Simpson, and Toni Braxton, for example. It's often difficult to distinguish between a lawyer working as a manager and a manager who also happens to be a lawyer, but it's a potential avenue to pursue as an alternate or in addition to finding an agent or traditional manager to represent you.

Publicists

When just getting started in the industry, it may not be cost-effective or even a good idea to consult a publicist or PR firm, but down the road, as you put together performances and products to market and publicize, publicists will likely be a major team player in the business of you.

Publicists must not only be effective in generating publicity, but also be effective in helping to manage your public persona. The primary manager of your public persona, however, is and always will be *you,* and again, the best kind of persona to have is one of integrity.

Advisors

To a certain extent, all of your professional service team members will be considered advisors. However, you'll also need to make sure that you surround yourself with people who specialize in advising.

This part of your team will likely be far less formal, though there are many wonderful professional advising resources out there to take advantage of. Consider me one of them. I wrote this book and became involved in education for aspiring entertainers because I saw a major void in decent, experience-based, agenda-free information.

Some of the best advisors out there can be found through continuing education programs. It was from a continuing education course that I took through the Learning Annex in New York that I learned exactly what I needed to know about copyrights, patents, trademarks, and music royalties from one of entertainment's top practicing lawyers. It only cost me $50 and about three hours of my time, but when it came to negotiating my first album, I estimate that the knowledge I gained in that course saved me no less than $100,000. That's a 2000 percent return on investment!

There are also a ton of great seminars out there, though there is definitely a mixed bag of quality, ranging from life-changing to lousy, with the only common denominator usually being a fairly large price tag for most of them. Luckily, most of the folks giving these expensive seminars are also authors who have, like me, put all of the exact same information in their book or books. If you're willing to read, you can save yourself several thousand dollars just by picking up a book for a few bucks!

One of the greatest resources for a top-quality advisor will ultimately be your own industry networking, and it's not out of the realm of possibility to someday have direct access to a leader in your field that you could ask for advice. Just remember to always be thorough and discriminatory in deciding (ultimately with your gut) who is in a worthy position to offer sound guidance.

Rule 16: Begin assembling your entertainment dream team.

ACTION 4:

Change Your Friends— Change Your Life

He who walks with wise men will be wise, but the companion of fools will suffer harm.

—Proverbs 13:20

A remarkable thing usually happens when a young person who's been in and out of trouble his whole life enlists in the military. Before long, a change takes place and the kid who used to follow the lowest common denominator in the neighborhood down the path of chaos becomes a high-functioning and disciplined leader.

Take that same person back out of the military environment and throw him back into the same neighborhood, and all too frequently that same "military leader" becomes a follower again and ends up in trouble. I've watched this exact cycle happen to several kids from my high school.

Similarly, countless studies have been conducted over the past several decades to discover how to break the cycle of incarceration for repeat offenders, and nearly every single study cites *environment* as a leading factor in determining whether or not reform is possible. In other words, change the criminal's environment, namely the people he is surrounded by, and you will literally change his life!

Analogously, the first thing alcoholics are told to do in recovery is to cut ties altogether with their drinking buddies. Smokers trying to quit smoking are encouraged to cut ties with their smoking friends. Simply put, we are who we surround ourselves with. So why not surround ourselves with the best?

The Takeaway

This may come as a harsh reality check, but most people end up no more successful than the people they choose to surround themselves with. By the same token, if you want to be successful, surround yourself with people who are already successfully doing what you want to do yourself.

Oprah Winfrey didn't really start to thrive until age fourteen, when she was sent to live with her father in Nashville, Tennessee, escaping the negative environment that contributed to her sister's cocaine addiction (which eventually took her life) and a brother who also died far too young, also an addict. At Oprah's new high school, she joined the speech team and began winning competitions, and she eventually won an oratory contest that secured her a full scholarship to Tennessee State University.

Harrison Ford became a high-end carpenter in LA, doing work for the biggest names in Hollywood. Ford was building cabinets for film director George Lucas when Lucas offered him a supporting role in his film *American Graffiti*.

Francis Ford Coppola was so impressed with the cabinetwork Ford did in Lucas's home that he hired Ford to expand his office . . . and then he gave him a small role in his film *The Conversation*.

One year later, Lucas asked Ford to help him cast roles in *Star Wars* by reading opposite other actors auditioning for the parts. He was so impressed by Ford's portrayal of Han Solo during these reads that he ended up hiring him for his career-making starring role.

In Oprah's case, fate played a large role in changing the environment that contributed greatly to her success. In Harrison Ford's case, he found himself in the right environment simply by building cabinets in the same room as George Lucas.

These stories represent the opportunity that most aspiring artists have to put ourselves into the right place at the right time and have the environment do a lot of our heavy lifting for us. Being surrounded by high achievers and shakers and movers not only helps when these same people are looking around for new blood to hire, it also significantly raises our own game.

On the speech team, Oprah was challenged by other high-performing students to stretch and do better. In college, she was surrounded by people who were ambitious and were going places and so, in part by assimilation, she did too.

As my parents always taught me, if you want to be better at sports, play against people better than you; a better writer, read books by great authors; better at anything, find the best and join them. Surround yourself, both physically and mentally, with high achievers. You simply can't do this if you're always too busy wasting your time with people who waste *your* time.

This isn't about not remembering your roots—after all, few celebrities are as connected to their roots and use their power to support them more than Oprah. This is about not making excuses and about choosing action over comfort.

Go

The inescapable reality of the entertainment industry is that for each discipline there are just a few physical locations that, if you want to have a career, you will need to physically go to. There, you will not only find access to career opportunities that you won't find anywhere else, but you'll also be surrounded by those who are already doing what you want to do, and you will learn a lot from them fast.

While there are certainly opportunities in most major cities and even smaller communities to get a start in most disciplines, you will eventually need to go to where the hub of your discipline lives and breathes in order to further your career.

If you're interested in film acting, you'll likely need to go to LA; theatre, New York City; songwriting, Nashville, Tennessee. These are just three of the most obvious examples. This reality is nearly inescapable, and embracing it will only speed your cause along as just about everyone at the top of his or her game had to make the move at some point too.

I chose New York City because it offered opportunities in just about every discipline. Though arguably not as strong as LA's film and TV scene, it was a hub for every artistic endeavor imaginable. Ultimately, I chose it primarily for the *quantity* of opportunities over quality.

As an aspiring ten-year-old recording artist, Dolly Parton lived in Sevierville, Tennessee. Her uncle, Billy Earl Owens, would regularly drive her several hours to recording studios in Knoxville and into Nashville to perform. In her autobiography, *Dolly: My Life and Other Unfinished Business,* she says this often meant waking up at 4:00 in the morning and even sleeping overnight in the car. But Nashville wasn't about to go to Sevierville to find her, and neither will Hollywood, Broadway, or Music Row come find you.

Once you are in these places, your creativity and networking skills will determine the type of successful people you come to be surrounded by. It may not have been entirely calculated that Harrison Ford found himself in a room at George Lucas's home, surrounded high-powered movie producers and casting directors . . . but if it was calculated, it was genius on his part.

Once Oprah experienced the opportunities that came from being in a supportive and competitive high school environment, she actively pursued greater challenges and greater achievers to associate with. Her landmark TV show, *Oprah,* became just another continuation of this habit, as week after week she invited some of the greatest achievers of all time into her studio and onto her couch so that she and her viewers could learn from them.

Go Virtual

It's obviously not always going to be possible to physically surround yourself with people at the top of their game. This is why, as I have asserted over and over in this book already, it is so critical to study them, which is the second best thing, and this resource is available to *everyone.*

Take a Good Look Around

Now . . . the hard part. I've already outlined some of the most common traps that many talented artists fall into, such as the subsistence job social trap. I've talked about a few types of people you'd be well served to avoid and/or cut ties with: wounded birds, scene stealers, distracters, rotten family, and salespeople.

Now it's time for you to decide who you want to be. Some folks are just more comfortable being comfortable. Risk and change is not in their DNA, and the fear of addressing unhealthy relationships and the role they play in them far outweighs their desire to become a celebrated artist. That's OK. Like I said earlier, this business is not for everybody.

But if you want to have a successful career in entertainment, you will need to put yourself in the game. That means surrounding yourself with people who are in the game, if you aren't doing that already . . . and getting away from people who are holding you back, if you haven't done *that* already.

Rule 17: Surround yourself physically and virtually with people who are achieving the things you desire.

The sooner you start this process, the sooner you will find success. So go ahead and take a good look around you, and begin!

I look forward to being entertained by you!

Gratefully,
Evan

RESOURCES

Success Literature

Anderson, U. S. *Three Magic Words: The Key to Power, Peace and Plenty* (California: Wilshire Book Company, 1977).

Butler-Bowdon, Tom. *50 Success Classics: Winning Wisdom for Life and Work from 50 Landmark Books* (London: Nicholas Brealey Publishing, 2007).

Byrne, Rhonda. *The Secret* (New York: Atria Books, 2006).

Canfield, Jack, with Janet Switzer. *The Success Principles: How to Get from Where You Are to Where You Want to Be* (New York: Harper Resource Book, 2005).

Chin-Ning, Chu. *Thick Face, Black Heart* (London: Nicholas Brealy Publishng, 1995).

Chopra, Deepak, M.D. *The Seven Spiritual Laws of Success: A Practical Guide to the Fulfillment of Your Dreams* (San Rafael, Calif.: Amber-Allen Publishing, New World Library, 1994).

Dyer, Wayne W. *Manifest Your Destiny: The Nine Spiritual Principles for Getting Everything You Want* (New York: HarperCollins Publishers, 1997).

Gladwell, Malcolm. *Outliers: The Story of Success* (New York: Little, Brown and Co., 2008).

Hill, Napoleon. *Think and Grow Rich* (Mineola, NY: Dover Publications, 2007).

Pink, Daniel H. *Drive: The Surprising Truth About What Motivates Us* (New York: Riverhead Books, 2011).

Robbins, Anthony. *Awaken the Giant Within: How to Take Immediate Control of Your Mental, Emotional, Physical and Financial Destiny!* (New York: Free Press, 1992).

Robbins, Anthony. *Unlimited Power: The New Science of Personal Achievement* (New York: Free Press, 1986).

Thomas, Peter H. *Be Great: the Five Foundations of an Extraordinary Life* (Brentwood, TN: Franklin Green Publishing, 2010).

Trump, Donald with Bill Zanker. *Think Big and Kick Ass in Business And Life* (New York: HarperCollins, 2007).

Success Skills

Burt, Gabor George. *Slingshot: Re-Imagine Your Business Re-Imagine Your Life* (Brentwood, TN: Franklin Green Publishing, 2010).

Carnegie, Dale. *How to Win Friends and Influence People* (New York, Simon and Schuster, 1936). *Note:* This book has been reprinted many times in many different editions. All are equally helpful!

Covey, Stephen R. *The 7 Habits Of highly Effective People* (New York: Free Press, 1989).

Covey, Stephen R., A. Roger Merrill, Rebecca R. Merrill. *First Things First: To Live, to Love, to Learn, to Leave a Legacy* (New York: Simon & Schuster, 1994).

Crenshaw, Dave. *The Myth of Multitasking: How "Doing It All" Gets Nothing Done* (San Francisco: Jossey-Bass, 2008).

Gardner, Daniel. *The Science of Fear: How the Culture of Fear Manipulates Your Brain* (New York: Plume, 2009).

Lorayne, Harry & Lucas Jerry. *The Memory Book: The Classic Guide to Improving Your Memory at Work, at School, and at Play* (New York: Ballantine Books, 1996).

Ries, Al & Laura Ries. *The 22 Immutable Laws of Branding* (New York: Harper Business, 2002).

Vaynerchuk, Gary. *Crush It!: Why NOW Is the Time to Cash In on Your Passion* (New York: HarperStudio, 2009).

Financial, Investing, and Asset Protection

Bach, David. *The Automatic Millionaire: A Powerful One-Step Plan to Live and Finish Rich* (New York: Broadway Books, 2004).

Bailey, Adam Leitman. *Finding the Uncommon Deal: A Top New York Lawyer Explains How to Buy a Home for the Lowest Possible Price* (Hoboken, NJ: John Wiley & Sons, Inc, 2011).

Ferriss, Timothy. *The 4-Hour Workweek: Escape 9–5, Live Anywhere, and Join the New Rich* (New York: Crown Publishers, 2007).

Kiyosaki, Robert, with Sharon L. Lecter, C.P.A. *Rich Dad Poor Dad: What the Rich Teach Their Kids About Money—That the Poor and Middle Class Do Not!* (New York: Business Plus, 2000).

Lechter, Sharon L. & Garrett Sutton. *Real Estate Advantages* (New York: Warner Business Books, 2006).

Pilzer, Paul Zane. *Unlimited Wealth: The Theory and Practice of Economic Alchemy* (New York: Crown Publishers, 1990).

Ramsey, Dave. *The Total Money Makeover: A Proven Plan for Financial Fitness* (Nashville: Thomas Nelson Pub., 2003).

Stanley, Thomas & William Danko. *The Millionaire Next Door: The Surprising Secrets of America's Wealthy* (New York: Pocket Books, 1996).

Sutton, Garrett, Esq. *Own Your Own Corporation: Why the Rich Own Their Own Companies and Everyone Else Works for Them* (New York: Warner Books, Inc., 2001).

Autobiographies & Biographies

Here are just a few favorite books from my personal collection. When looking them up online to find out if they were still in print I ran across no fewer than one hundred more biographies and autobiographies that I plan on reading, and many that, frankly, I wish I had read long ago—even though in some cases they had yet to be written back then!

When I was starting out in this business, my most valued investment was a monthly subscription to *Biography* magazine. Sadly, it is no longer in print, but you can search the Internet and find a million interviews from just about anyone in the public eye.

An autobiography, however, is special in that it gives the kind of depth and nuance of a lifetime of decisions, risks, and rewards from the perspective of the person who made those decisions, took those risks, and reaped those rewards. Given the choice, I will always prefer reading books actually written by those who have lived the life being written about—to me, those are the words that will always provide the biggest insight to success.

Abagnale, Frank W., Redding, Stan. *Catch Me If You Can: The True Story of a Real Fake* (New York: Grosset & Dunlap, 1980).

Cameron, James. *James Cameron: Interviews,* edited by Brent Dunham (Jackson: University Press of Mississippi, 2012).

Chenoweth, Kristin with Joni Rodgers. *A Little Bit Wicked: Life, Love, and Faith in Stages* (New York: Simon & Schuster, 2009).

Fox, Michael J. *Lucky Man: A Memoir* (New York: Hyperion, 2002).

Frankl, Viktor E. *Man's Search for Meaning* (Boston: Beacon Press, 1962).

Jordan, Michael, and Mark Vancil. *Driven from Within* (New York: Atria Books, 2005).

Judd, Ashley, with Maryanne Vollers. *All That Is Bitter & Sweet: A Memoir* (New York: Ballantine Books, 2011).

Kelley, Kitty. *Oprah: A Biography* (New York: Crown Publishers, 2010).

Lowe, Rob. *Stories I Only Tell My Friends: An Autobiography* (New York: Henry Holt and Co., 2011).

Martin, Steve. *Born Standing Up: A Comic's Life* (New York: Scribner, 2007).

McBride, Joseph. *Steven Spielberg: A Biography,* 2nd ed. (Jackson: University Press of Mississippi, 2010).

Paisley, Brad, with David Wild. *Diary of a Player: How My Musical Heroes Made a Guitar Man Out of Me* (New York: Howard Books, 2011).

Parton, Dolly. *Dolly: My Life and Other Unfinished Business* (New York: Harper Collins, 1994).

Swayze, Patrick, Lisa Niemi. *The Time of My Life* (New York: Atria Books, 2009).

Tyler, Steven. *Does That Noise in My Head Bother You? A Rock 'n' Roll Memoir* (New York: Ecco Press, 2011).

Walters, Barbara. *Audition: A Memoir* (New York: A.A. Knopf, 2008).

ABOUT THE AUTHOR

To Evan Farmer, there is no such thing as a "Bucket List" . . . only things that he's either done, doing, or going to do. That's the mantra that has guided Evan in his extremely diverse, accomplished, and eclectic path—whether it's finding success in nearly every genre of the entertainment industry, building an airplane in eleven days and then flying it solo across the country, starting businesses, writing, teaching, traveling, or helping to further charities that are meaningful to him.

Evan attributes his career in entertainment, one in which he has worked consistently for nearly two decades—in music, major concert venues, theatre, television, film, print, and radio—to his unbridled passion for adventure and to a compulsion for continuously challenging himself in literally every arena that peaks his interests. If there's one characteristic that defines Evan the most, however, it's his love affair with learning and sharing what he has learned with great enthusiasm.

Evan resides in Nashville, Tennessee, with his wife Andrea; their two sons, Garrison and Ford; and their devoted rescue dog, Sally.